John Anderson.
Duns.
July, 1939.

Law Lectures to Bankers

Law Lectures to Bankers

BY

ROBERT FINLAYSON

WRITER, GLASGOW

LECTURER TO THE INSTITUTE OF BANKERS IN SCOTLAND
1934, 1935, 1937

*Reproduced by request of the Council
of the Institute*

William Blackwood & Sons Limited
Edinburgh and London
1939

PREFACE

THESE Lectures, delivered between 1934 and 1938
to the Institute of Bankers in Scotland and now
brought up to date, were specially prepared for
the guidance of their members in relation to some
of the more practical aspects of their business and
do not pretend to cover anything more than a
part of the law of banking in Scotland.

The endeavour was to treat in simple non-
technical form and language certain selected
matters which frequently arise for consideration
in banking business and which, to some extent,
had not previously been dealt with in detail from
the practical side in the text-books on the subject.

To the Institute I acknowledge the honour
which they have done me in inviting me to put
before their members in this form some of the
principal rules of law relating to the active conduct
of their business and the results of a long experience
in the application of these in daily practice. To
Mr F. H. Allan, the Secretary of the Institute, I
am indebted for counsel and assistance always
willingly and kindly given not only in the preparation and delivery of the Lectures but also in the

preparation of this volume for the press. To the local Secretaries and Officials of the Institute my thanks are due for help in many ways, and to my partners and assistants I owe a debt of gratitude for their collaboration without which this work would not have been possible.

R. F.

172 St Vincent Street, Glasgow.
April 1939.

CONTENTS

INDEX OF CASES.

ix

Index of Cases

Index of Cases

Index of Cases

The Law of Bills, Cheques and
Deposit Receipts

LECTURE I.

THE law relating to bills and cheques is to be found mainly in the Bills of Exchange Acts of 1882, 1906, 1917 and 1932, the Stamp Act of 1853, the Revenue Act of 1883, the Stamp Act of 1891, and in the reports of many decided cases. These Acts relate to England as well as to Scotland, but most of the cases are English, and while the law in general is the same in both countries, there are important differences to which I shall refer later on. Practically all the text-books are English, but, in the present circumstances, I propose to deal with the subject only from our own local point of view.

Dealing with the subject of cheques in the first instance, you are all familiar with the definition given in the 1882 Act, and I would merely remind you that the essentials of a cheque are that it must be in writing and drawn on a banker; it must be unconditional; it must be for a definite specified sum, and it must be signed by the drawer and be payable to or to the order of a specified person or to bearer. Unless the cheque complies with all the various requirements of the 1882 Act it does not carry with it any of the privileges accorded to such a document, or the protection intended for bankers handling it.

Three sections of the 1882 Act are of great importance to you.

1

A

Sec. 60, you will recollect, provides immunity to the paying banker in respect of the indorsement of cheques payable to order on demand and which are paid by him in good faith and in the ordinary course of business. A similar, but somewhat wider, immunity is provided by sec. 19 of the Stamp Act of 1853 to cover any draft or order drawn upon a banker payable to order on demand.

Sec. 80 gives the paying banker a similar immunity as regards crossed cheques which he pays to another banker in good faith and without negligence, and sec. 82 protects the collecting banker who, in good faith and without negligence, receives payment of a crossed cheque for a customer of his. These last two sections have been extended by sec. 17 of the Revenue Act of 1883 to cover any document issued by a customer of any banker, and intended to enable any person to obtain from such banker payment of the sum mentioned in it, but the last-mentioned section does not make such a document a negotiable instrument.

The drafts or orders or cheques which you handle day by day are anything but uniform either in form or legal effect. Most of them probably fall within the definition of a cheque in the 1882 Act ; others fall under the 1853 Act or, if crossed, under the 1883 Act, while others fall under no Act but are regulated by common law. If you were to examine your paid cheques or drafts or orders at the close of a single day's business, and apply to them the tests provided by the 1882 Act, you would probably be surprised at the proportion not falling under that Act and the risks which you are taking because you do not have the protection afforded by it.

A few words will serve to give an idea of what these risks may be. For example :—

1. It is only under the 1882 Act that you can be a holder in due course with a better title than the person from whom you took the document.
2. Sec. 60 of the 1882 Act and sec. 19 of the 1853 Act apply only to cheques payable to order on demand. Many cheques to-day are not payable to order and are really not transferable, if they are properly read.

If in any respect a cheque does not come within the Acts you require to rely upon your common law rights—whatever these may be. Our common law as regards these matters is not so very well developed as to be entirely relied upon by you or explained by me, and the most I can say at present is that when you leave what might be termed the solid highway of statutory authority, your path is likely to be a difficult one.

In addition to the requirements of the 1882 Act, a cheque must bear a 2d. stamp in terms of the Stamp Act of 1891, unless where exemption has been given as in the case of Friendly Societies, trustees in bankruptcy, government departments, and so on, and if a form of receipt is to be completed on the cheque, a 2d. receipt stamp is required on that if for £2 or over, even although the cheque itself may be exempt from duty. A post-dated cheque is liable only in duty as a bill payable on demand, although it may be said to be in effect a bill drawn at a currency. You will see that that is so later on when we come to deal with the presentment of a cheque operating as an ntimated assignation in favour of the holder.

In drawing a cheque on his bank account, a customer has certain duties to perform not only towards his banker but also towards the payee, to say nothing of a duty to himself, and in the event of his failure to observe care in doing so, he himself must take the responsibility for any loss which may arise therefrom. Two cases will be sufficient to illustrate the customer's position in this matter.

The first is the well-known case of the *London Joint Stock Bank* v. *Macmillan & Arthur* (1918, A.C. 777), where a cheque in an incomplete form was negligently signed by the customer for a sum of apparently £2, and was fraudulently altered by his clerk to read as if it had been drawn for £120. In giving judgment for the bank, who had paid £120 on the cheque and debited the customer's account accordingly, the House of Lords held that a customer is bound to exercise reasonable care to prevent his banker being misled. If he draws a cheque in a manner which facilitates fraud, he is guilty of a breach of duty as between himself and the banker, and he is responsible to the banker for any loss sustained by the banker as a natural and direct consequence of this breach of duty.

The other case relating to the customer's duty to the payee is that of *Robb* v. *Gow Bros. & Gemmell* (1905, 8 F. 90). There an uncrossed bearer cheque was posted by the bank's customer to his stock-brokers to settle the price of some shares which the latter had purchased for him. The cheque reached the stockbrokers' office all right, but there it was stolen and cashed by one of the stockbrokers' clerks. The brokers took up the position that payment of the price of the shares had not been received by them from their client, and they declined to hand over to him the share certificate. The Court held that the client had failed to observe the recognised precautions for ensuring that a

4

cheque sent by post should actually reach the payee, and that the loss in this case had been occasioned by his negligence and should be borne by him.

As a contrast to this case, attention may be drawn to *Ode Gesellschaft, &c.* v. *Jewish Colonial Trust* (1927, 43 T.L.R. 398), where a draft, sent by the defendants to Rumania, went amissing and was paid in Poland on a forged indorsement, and Mr Justice MacKinnon held that the defendants were not negligent in not having the draft insured.

From these cases it is obvious that a customer in drawing a cheque must do so in such a way as on the one hand not to mislead his banker, and on the other not to deprive the payee of the normal measure of protection to which he is entitled, otherwise the loss arising from his negligence must be borne by himself. Where, however, there is no negligence attributable to the customer, and his cheque is fraudulently altered, the position is different.

If, for example, the amount for which a cheque has been drawn without fault or negligence has been fraudulently altered so as to increase the amount originally intended to be paid, the banker will be responsible and will only be entitled to debit his customer's account with the original amount.

Sec. 64 relates to the case of a cheque being altered in any material particular—such as an alteration in the amount, &c.,—and provides that such cheque is altogether void unless where the alteration is not apparent and the cheque is in the hands of a holder in due course. Such holder in due course may enforce payment of the cheque, but only to the extent of the original amount or, in the words of the Act, according to its original tenor.

An example of this position is to be found in

Slingsby v. *The District Bank* (1932, 1 K.B. 544), where a cheque drawn in favour of J. P. & Co. or order by certain executors was handed by them to their solicitor for transmission to the payees. The solicitor instead of doing so altered the cheque by adding after J. P. & Co. the words per C. & B. (the name of his own firm), indorsed the cheque C. & B. and misappropriated the amount. The executors objected to the cheque being debited to their account, and in an action against the bank they were successful on the ground that the cheque had been fraudulently altered by the solicitor in a material particular. At the same time the Court held that in drawing that cheque the executors had not been guilty of negligence merely because the space for the payees' name had not been completely utilised or struck through. Later on, I propose to refer to this case again in connection with the responsibilities of the collecting and paying banker.

A cheque in terms of the Act must be drawn payable on demand. No cheque, however, expresses that it is payable on demand. It reads simply " Pay to A. B. the sum of £," but sec. 10 of the Act provides that a bill, which, of course, includes a cheque, is payable on demand where no time for payment is expressed in it. A cheque is to be regarded as none the less payable on demand even where, as in the form of a dividend warrant, it requires to be presented before a given date, or where, as in the case of a post-dated cheque, it cannot be paid until after a given date.

A cheque must also be unconditional. This is a requirement which, in certain circumstances, has given rise to doubt and uncertainty, and there is a real lack of authoritative guidance on many points.

To take an extreme case, assume you are presented with an uncrossed cheque which reads : " Pay to A. or order the sum of £ provided the receipt below is duly signed." The terms of the receipt are immaterial. Obviously, that is a conditional cheque—*i.e.*, conditional upon the receipt being signed, and, as such, is outwith the Act altogether.

You will notice in the first place that this cheque is payable to order and there is no apparent indication of any prohibition against its being transferred. How then can it be dealt with, and what rights or responsibilities pertain to the bankers who handle it ?

Apparently A. can pass on the cheque to B., but is that to be done by A. simply completing the form of receipt and handing the document over or must A. also put the usual indorsement on the back as well as sign the receipt ? Alternatively, is A. simply to put the usual indorsement on the back leaving B. to complete the form of receipt ? These are matters on which no guidance is given on the cheque.

If the receipt only is completed by A., what rights will B. acquire on the document being handed over to him ? There is nothing to show any transference to him of the property in the cheque and he cannot be a holder in due course as the cheque, being conditional, is outside the Act, so that he would appear to be really only an agent or messenger entrusted by A. with the duty of collecting payment of the amount.

If, in addition to the receipt being completed, A. has indorsed the cheque before delivery, B. would have an apparent title of some kind to the property in the cheque, but, as the document is outside the Act, he thereby gets no better right than A. had.

7

The banker collecting such a cheque for B. and the banker paying it on behalf of the drawer are not protected against the usual risks and are responsible in every respect for acting strictly in accordance with the drawer's mandate contained in the cheque. Further, if B. has merely signed the receipt without indorsing the cheque, the collecting banker is merely an agent for collection and cannot possibly be a holder in due course.

A cheque such as that just instanced, which is clearly conditional and so not covered by the Act, while involving its own awkward possibilities, is not so difficult to construe as the troublesome class where there is a doubt as to whether the requirements of the form do or do not make it a conditional cheque. Each document of this class falls to be considered on its own merits, but a general rule has been laid down to the effect that where the instructions or requirements appearing on the cheque are intended for the banker, the cheque is probably conditional, but, if such instructions or requirements are intended for the payee, the cheque is probably unconditional. This distinction, however, is elusive and unsatisfactory.

The cases in this class are too numerous to permit of detailed consideration here, but I would like to say a few words with regard to two of the better known.

In one of them there is a form of receipt indorsed on the back of the cheque and reads : " Received from X. Co. Ltd. the sum mentioned on the face hereof." Then follows the signature of the payee immediately above a note, reading : " This signature is intended to be an indorsement of this cheque as well as a receipt for the amount."

In the other, a form of receipt is printed at the bottom of the cheque, reading : " Received the above-mentioned sum," followed by the signature of the payee and a note, reading : "No further receipt is necessary and no indorsement of this cheque is required."

As regards cases like these I cannot do better than quote the opinion of Sir John Paget, who says :—

"Even if the requirements as to the signature of the receipt are not such as to make the cheque conditional, it is submitted that such signature cannot serve the double purpose of receipt and indorsement ; it is not made solely *animo indorsandi*, or delivered as an indorsement, and a banker paying it runs the risk of liability in case the signature is a forgery and that, if crossed, the collecting banker is outside sec. 82."

And again :—

"It is submitted that the signature of the receipt is not an effective indorsement. There is no legal authority that indorsement can be effected by a signature which fulfils another end. The *animus indorsandi* can hardly be predicted in such case. It would, therefore, seem that such signature would not give the paying banker protection under sec. 60 if it proved to be a forgery."

If the payee of such a cheque signs the receipt thereon, and then negotiates it to B. on an indorsement reading, say : "Pay to B. or order," the absurd inconsistency of the position is at once emphasised, because what the indorsement in effect says is really this : Notwithstanding the terms of the foregoing receipt, I have *not* received the above-mentioned sum, but I assign my right to receive it to B. Conversely, if the receipt means what it says—that is, that the payee *has* received the money—what is there left to transfer or indorse to B. ?

While the two forms of cheque with receipt annexed last-mentioned might be regarded as unconditional when read by themselves, the Courts as a rule will look at all the facts and circumstances. In the general case a customer who issues cheques of this nature usually does so under an arrangement with his banker, whereby the banker is instructed to refuse payment of any such cheque where the receipt has not been signed and the customer agrees to indemnify and keep the banker clear. If, in a case coming before the Courts with regard to such a cheque, this arrangement or instruction is disclosed, the Court might probably, in view of the terms of sec. 100, have little difficulty in reading the cheque and the banker's separate instructions together as one, and finding that the cheque was, notwithstanding its apparently unconditional terms, really a conditional cheque and so outside the Act altogether.

The document usually taken by a banker who agrees to his customer using cheques with a receipt form appended, runs in something like the following terms—the forms used by all our banks are not alike, but I quote an actual case :—

" GENTLEMEN,—In consideration of your allowing us to draw cheques on you which have printed on the back thereof a form of receipt, the signature to which is intended to operate also as an indorsement, we hereby agree and declare that you shall have the same protection and rights in all respects as if the cheques had been unconditional drafts or bills payable to order on demand ; and that the signature of the said receipt shall in each case have the same effect and give you the same protection as if it had been an indorsement of the cheque purporting to be made by the person to whom it is drawn payable. Further, we authorise and request you to return or refuse payment of any cheque the receipt whereon is incomplete in any respect, and we undertake to keep you free from all liability in respect of your doing so."

You will notice that this document says that the paying banker is to have the same protection and rights in all respects as if these cheques had been unconditional. The clear inference from that is that these cheques are conditional and so outside the Act.

You will also notice that the document says that the receipt is to have the same effect and give the paying banker the same protection as if it had been an indorsement. Again, the clear inference is that the receipt is not an indorsement.

This document is addressed to the banker on whom the cheques are drawn, and whatever protection is given by it is given to him alone, and to no one else. To all others these cheques apparently remain conditional, and carry none of the privileges of the Act.

If, therefore, you are collecting the amount of such a cheque for a customer, and find, on putting it through the clearing, that the banker on whom it is drawn has been instructed to stop payment thereof, you have no rights as against the drawer. Even although the cheque has been indorsed by the payee, as well as having the receipt form completed, you are in no better position, because you are outside the Act, and it is only under the Act that you can be a holder in due course with a better title than your customer.

Your only remedy is against your own customer, for whom you are collecting, and if he is financially sound you will probably be able to recover the amount as against him. If not, the loss will be yours.

A nice question may, however, arise between you and your customer—the payee—even although he is good for the money if he takes up the position that, not having indorsed the cheque, he is not liable to you thereon. This is somewhat similar to the question which arises in a case where you receive for collection a bearer cheque which does

11

not require indorsement, and in fact is not indorsed, but is returned to you unpaid for some reason or another. The position between your customer and yourself is just a little difficult, and will depend upon the whole facts and circumstances of the transaction, but the obvious course to follow is to have all bearer cheques indorsed by your customer, and to have all composite cheques, with receipts thereon, indorsed in addition to having the receipts signed.

While on this subject I should perhaps draw your attention to sec. 31 (4) of the Act, under which it is provided that where the holder of a bill or cheque payable to his order transfers it for value without indorsing it, the transfer gives the transferee such title as the transferor had in the bill or cheque, and the transferee in addition acquires the right to have the indorsement of the transferor. This presumably is the position where a composite cheque is handed over with merely the receipt thereon completed. If, therefore, it is correct to say that the signature of the receipt is not an indorsement, then there is no legal transfer of the property in the cheque. There is also sec. 55 (2), which provides that an indorser, by indorsing a bill or cheque, engages that, on due presentment, it will be paid, and that if it be dishonoured he will compensate the holder or his indorsee. The benefit of this provision is, of course, lost if there has been no indorsement, either of a bearer cheque or of a composite cheque with receipt form appended. Again, under sec. 58, where the holder of a bill or cheque payable to bearer negotiates it by delivery without indorsing it, he is not liable on the instrument, and under sec. 23 no person is liable as an indorser who has not signed as such.

In these circumstances it would seem desirable that serious consideration should be given to the question whether the use of composite cheques of the kind referred to should not be stopped altogether, or the practice with regard thereto regularised in some way. The completion of the receipt form serves no useful purpose, as the simple indorsement of the payee is sufficient proof of his having received the money, while the use of such cheques is a danger to everyone handling them except perhaps the paying banker, who, however, by his covering letter protects himself but not the collecting banker.

As regards the payee, a cheque may be made payable to A., or to A. or order, or to A. or bearer. If it is made payable to A. simply, it is nevertheless payable to him or his order at his option and is negotiable accordingly.

A cheque may, however, be made payable to A. in such a way as to prevent him from negotiating or transferring it to anyone else, and that is where the benefit of sec. 60 is lost, because it is not a cheque payable to order—for example, a cheque drawn payable to A. only, the word " order " or " bearer " being deleted, and the words " not transferable " written across it. Such a restricted cheque cannot be crossed, as that would involve negotiation or transfer to a banker, and that is apparently just what is intended should not take place.

The restrictions with regard to the payee, which are becoming fairly common, are more or less an attempt on the part of the drawer to contract out of the Act and deprive his banker as well as the collecting banker of the protection to which they are normally entitled under the Act. I refer to cheques made payable to A. only, cheques

13

marked " not transferable " and " account payee only," and I propose to refer to this aspect in my next lecture when dealing with the indorsement and negotiation of cheques.

One particular cheque of this kind I have in mind at the moment is a special one printed by a bank in the usual way and issued to their customers for use by them. The printed parts of the cheque include the words " or order," two parallel transverse lines, the words " & Co.," " not negotiable," and " account payee only." The only writing on the cheque is the name of the payee and the amount, with, of course, the drawer's signature and date.

It is difficult to understand how any bank came to issue a cheque like that. I feel sure they do not know what it means. At any rate I cannot tell you. It says at one place that it is payable to order, and at another place that it is not payable to order.

It is all very well for the bank who issue cheques like that to ignore the legal implications, because they are no doubt protected by the covering letter or agreement which they hold from their customers and which authorises them to debit to the account all cheques of this kind without question when paid. I wish you, however, to pay particular attention to the position of the collecting banker handling such a cheque, and to consider what his rights in the cheque can be.

The point about this particular form of cheque is that it is used by an insurance company who pay out considerable sums to claimants for compensation or damages in respect of third party claims, running-down accidents and so on. The cheques are usually made payable to the claimant himself and are sent by post to his solicitor. In

14

practically all these cases the claimant has no bank account, and the only thing that can be done with such a cheque is to get him to indorse it and then to have it indorsed by his solicitor and paid into the credit of the solicitor's own account. Of course this, on the face of it, is wrong, and while bankers as a rule are prepared to accept certain risks in this way, it seems to me, having regard to this particular class of business, that extra precautions are necessary to avoid claims on the ground of conversion, negligence and so on.

Inconsistencies like these in the drawing of a cheque should be discouraged wherever possible, and it would seem only reasonable on the part of a paying banker that when he takes a covering letter or agreement with regard to the issue of cheques of this kind, he should endeavour to do something to protect not only himself but also any collecting banker who acts in good faith in the matter.

A cheque may be made payable to " the executors of A." or to " the legal personal representatives of A." without their being named. This is done in connection with the settlement of newspaper insurance claims where prompt payment, so called, is made a feature of the scheme. Extrinsic evidence is admissible in a case of this kind to show precisely who the executors or legal personal representatives are, but the only evidence which you can accept is the Confirmation in their favour. A.'s Will by itself will not do, and if Confirmation has not yet been taken out the cheque cannot be paid until that has been done. There is no objection, however, to your clearing the cheque with your guarantee thereon, and putting the amount on deposit receipt in the same name or description as in the cheque to await production of the Confirmation.

A cheque may be made payable to any number of payees jointly, in which case an indorsement by all is required. It may, however, be made payable to any one or two or more of such payees, in which case, of course, an indorsement by the specified number only is required. On the other hand, it may be payable to several named persons jointly and severally when it is sufficiently indorsed by any one of them. In the case of a dividend warrant made payable to several joint holders, whether executors or otherwise, all should sign except where the warrant has been issued by an English company payable in England where the rule is different. In that case one signature, usually that of the first-named payee, is all that is required.

Under sec. 3 a cheque payable to order must be drawn payable to a specified person, which includes a body of persons whether incorporated or not. It cannot be drawn payable, for example, to " Wages or order " or " Cash or order," as that does not meet the requirement of a personal payee. A bearer cheque is different in this respect, and may be drawn payable to " Wages or bearer " and so on.

It was held in *North and South Insurance Corporation Ltd.* v. *National Provincial Bank Ltd.* (1936, 1 K.B. 328), that an order to pay to " cash or order " was not a cheque under the 1882 Act, but fell to be construed by intention, and that the bank was quite in order in paying cash to the bearer.

In connection with the insertion of the payee's name in a cheque, it is not uncommon for some customers to make the cheque read : " Pay to yourselves or order." That is a perfectly good cheque and authorises the bank to debit the amount to the customer's account, but that is all the length it goes. The question as to how you are to dispose of the money once you have taken it from the customer's account is another matter altogether. The fact that you have been so authorised to take the money out of the account does not entitle you to hand it over to your customer's messenger or alter its ownership in any way. The money still belongs to your customer, and you are accountable accordingly. Even in a case where your customer, wishing cash for himself, presents a cheque made payable to "yourselves or order," it is necessary for your own protection to obtain from him some evidence that the money was actually handed over to him, as otherwise he might deny having received it—which would, of course, be awkward, to say the least of it.

If, as is often intended in cases of this kind, the money so withdrawn from the customer's account is to be lodged on deposit receipt, it will be quite in order for you to make out such a deposit receipt provided it is for the full amount and is in name of your customer. If, however, only part of the money is to be put on deposit receipt, and the balance paid over in cash to your customer's messenger, then, in the absence of any special arrangement with your customer or well-recognised course of dealing with him, you should obtain your customer's specific instructions to that effect either in the cheque or otherwise.

The same position arises where the customer draws a cheque in favour of the bank to enable them to issue a draft. You must make sure that you have your customer's instructions as to whom the draft is to be made payable. It is not sufficient for the cheque to read: "Pay to yourselves for draft." It should read: "Pay to yourselves for draft to John Smith," because, as in the case of the *Bank of Montreal* v. *Dominion Gresham Guarantee & Casualty Co.* (1930, A.C. 659), it would be possible for the customer's messenger to get you to make out a draft in his own or some other name and deal with it fraudulently. The banker should, therefore, take nothing for granted, and in circumstances like these it is plainly negligence on the part of the banker to dispose of the money in such cheque unless on the clear instructions of the customer.

The principal remaining point in connection with the completion of a valid cheque is the signature of the drawer, which is of vital importance to a banker, as he does not have with regard to it the protection afforded to him under the Act as regards the signature of the payee.

If the signature of the drawer of a cheque be forged that cheque is a nullity and confers no rights upon anyone. A banker has no statutory or other protection in the event of his paying a cheque on which his customer's signature has been forged, and even although he has acted *bona fide* and without negligence he is not entitled to debit such a cheque to his customer's account.

If, however, the customer has been guilty of contributory negligence or, after becoming aware of the forgery, acts in such a manner as to indicate that he has adopted or approved of the forged signature or knowingly does something which misleads the banker or omits to do something which might obviate prejudice to the banker, he may be held as having acquiesced in the forgery and so be precluded from objecting to it. The case of *Greenwood* v. *Martins Bank* (1933, A.C. 51) is a good example of this. There a wife had forged

her husband's signature to cheques on his account
and, although he became aware of what she had
done, he took no steps for eight months.   On
his deciding to disclose the forgeries to the bank
the wife committed suicide.   He then sued the
bank for the loss of the money, but it was held
that he had failed in his duty to the bank and
by the delay prejudiced their position and consequently was not entitled to succeed.

When a banker has paid a cheque on which his
customer's signature has been forged and has no
remedy against his customer as above indicated,
the question at once arises as to whether he has
any right of relief against anyone else and, if so,
how it is to be enforced.   So far as Scotland is
concerned, there is practically no authority on
the subject and the text-books make no reference
to it.

The subject has been gone into in England,
however, more particularly with regard to bills,
but the cases are extremely conflicting and con-
fusing and really do not give a simple answer to
what appears to be a simple question.   In short,
it is difficult to say whether or not any of the
English cases have any bearing on the question
in Scotland because of differences in underlying
principles in the law of each country, and one is,
in the circumstances, naturally driven to consider
the whole question from a fresh point of view.

The right to repayment of money paid in mistake
depends upon the question whether the mistake
is a mistake in law or a mistake in fact.   If it was
by a mistake in law, there is no right to repayment,
as every person is presumed to know the law and
therefore cannot be mistaken about it.   On the
other hand, if it was by a mistake in fact, there
is a right to repayment, and in any case the general

rule is that stolen money can be followed and recovered.

It seems clear that a payment of the sum in a forged cheque is recoverable from the person to whom the payment was made. Such recovery will accordingly be from the forger himself or from an indorsee of his or perhaps from the collecting banker, and it is questionable whether it makes any difference that the person to whom the payment was made was acting merely as an agent for someone else or that he has in the meantime altered his position for the worse by parting with the money to his principal. In *The Clydesdale Bank* v. *The Royal Bank* (1876, 3 R. 586) the Court held the latter as collecting banker to be an agent only and so not responsible to refund the amount paid to them on the presentment of a forged cheque, but, from the facts as disclosed in the report of that case, I am doubtful as to whether it can be relied upon as an authority. The cases of *Starkey* v. *The Bank of England* (1903, A.C. 114), and *Sheffield Corporation* v. *Barclay* (1905, A.C. 392), clearly defining the liability of an agent for delivering a transfer which has, without his knowledge, been forged, seem to me to be equally applicable to an agent who delivers a forged cheque and obtains payment therefor.

To enable you to trace the person to whom the payment was made, and to compel him to admit responsibility to you in the matter, it is necessary that you have the document indorsed by him, not because an indorsement will transfer the property in the cheque to you—there is nothing to transfer in a case of this kind—but because you might not otherwise be able satisfactorily to bring the charge home to him. In this connection you will remember the observations made

20

above as to the indorsement of bearer cheques, which, according to the present practice, are not generally regarded as requiring indorsement, and also as to the indorsement of composite cheques with receipt forms appended.

These conclusions of mine as to right of recovery in respect of a forged cheque are not quite in accordance with the conclusions which have apparently been reached by eminent authorities in England on the same subject, and I accordingly submit them to you with great deference. The underlying principles are not quite the same in each country, and that may account for the apparent divergence.

Proceeding, however, with the signature of the cheque as the last act in its completion, it must be kept in view that this is of importance not only to the paying banker but to everyone handling the cheque. The payee and his indorsees have a very material interest in the authenticity of the signature, as they have to rely thereon in enforcing payment, if such a course should become necessary.

Quite a number of cheques are issued on which the customer's signature is not written by himself, but is adhibited in some other manner, and in cases of that kind the paying banker usually holds a covering letter authorising him to pay such cheques and debit them to the account without question. Such a letter, of course, protects the paying banker and no one else. All other persons handling such cheques must be prepared, in case of need, to bring home liability to the drawer in some other way.

Sec. 91 provides that it is sufficient if the drawer's signature is written by some other person by or under his authority, and that is exactly what a holder in due course must prove if he wishes to enforce payment from the drawer of a cheque, payment of which has been countermanded. Where the authority to sign cheques has been abused, it is sometimes a fine point as to whether or not the result is forgery, but, in any case, it would be very unsatisfactory for a holder in due course or a collecting banker in that position to have to face any question on this point.

I need not detain you with a list of the various possible forms adopted in the signature of cheques where the customer does not himself sign, or signs in some peculiar way, but perhaps it would not be out of place to suggest that the paying banker, when agreeing to the issue by his customer of cheques so authenticated, should endeavour, if at all practicable, to extend the protection afforded by his covering letter at least to the collecting banker.

A bank account may be opened in the joint names of two or more persons, in which case the cheques on the account will be signed by them all, unless the banker has received specific instructions, which should, of course, be in writing signed by all the parties, authorising cheques to be honoured when signed in some other way.

On the death or bankruptcy of one of the customers in a joint account, his executors or the trustee on his sequestrated estate must sign the cheques on the account along with the remaining customers, unless it has been otherwise stipulated at the opening of the account.

If it is contemplated in the case of a joint account in the name of two or more persons, that there should be or may be an overdraft, the banker is not entitled to rely upon such persons being jointly and severally responsible therefor,

even although all have signed the cheque or
cheques creating the debit. The case of *Coats* v.
The Union Bank (1929, S.C. H.L. 114) cleared up
that point. Shortly stated, the rule laid down by
the House of Lords in that case is that where
two or more persons draw a cheque on a joint
account, and the bank upon which it is drawn
pays that cheque, the cheque is discharged. A
bank which pays a cheque drawn on itself does
not thereby become the holder for value of that
cheque. After payment, the bank is confined to
suing on the obligation, express or implied, arising
out of the fact of their having made the payment,
and in the Coats case this was shown by the previous
correspondence to be a joint obligation only, as
the account on which the advance was to be made
had been referred to as a joint account. No
reference had been made expressly to a joint and
several liability. This confirms the necessity of
your taking a letter on the opening of a joint
account or the granting of an overdraft on such
an account under which the joint and several
liability of the customers is admitted for any
debit balance which may arise thereon.

Where, however, the cheque on a joint account
has not been met by the bank on which it is
drawn, but is in the hands of a holder in due
course, the position is different. Such holder in
due course is entitled to proceed against the
drawers jointly and severally for the amount
contained in it.

In the case of a joint account in name of A. and
B. and either or survivor, the question is sometimes
asked as to whether A. or B. alone can grant a
mandate or power of attorney in favour of a third
person to authorise him to sign cheques on the
account in place of A. or of B. It is not possible

to answer such a question without full knowledge of the facts, and, as a general rule, you should decline to act upon any such mandate or power of attorney.

The reason for this lies in the fact that when money is placed in bank in name of A. and B. and either or survivor, whether on current account or on deposit receipt, the ownership thereof is not regarded as having been changed thereby, and the presumption is that such a joint arrangement was made merely as a matter of convenience to the parties.

Consequently, on the death of A. or of B. the survivor no doubt has the sole right to withdraw the money in a question with the bank, but the beneficial ownership of the money remains as before. If, therefore, the money was really A.'s property, it may, on his death, be drawn out by B., but B. would require to account for it to A.'s executors. Obviously, therefore, while A. is alive B. alone could not give a valid mandate or power of attorney to another to operate on the account and so draw out A.'s money. On the same reasoning neither A. nor B. can, in the absence of special arrangement, overdraw the account so as to render the other liable for the debit.

It is different, however, in the case of a joint account in name of two or more persons as individuals where, according to the arrangement made when the account was opened, the cheques require to be signed by all. In such a case any one or more of these joint customers can grant a mandate or power of attorney in favour of a third person to sign the cheques in his place.

On the other hand, if, when the account was opened, the arrangement made was that the

24

cheques were to be signed by, say, any two out of four joint customers, no one of them is entitled to grant a mandate or power of attorney to any other person to sign in his place. The reason for this obviously is that each set of two of these joint customers are merely delegates of the whole, and accordingly are not entitled to sub-delegate their authority.

Where any mandate or power of attorney is presented to you in the case of a joint account, where such a mandate or power of attorney can properly be granted, you require to make certain that it really authorises the mandatory or attorney to operate on a bank account in which the granter is jointly interested with others. It is not sufficient to enable that to be done if the document merely authorises operations " on any bank account in my name " or other similar restrictive words.

Trustees or executors frequently find it necessary or desirable to open a bank account in connection with the administration of the estate under their charge. Apart from any special stipulation in the deed under which they act, the majority of them form a quorum and are accordingly entitled to sign the cheques on the account. At the opening of the account you should satisfy yourself as to who are the trustees or executors, and obtain a letter from them requesting the account to be opened and authorising you to honour cheques drawn thereon when signed by one or more or all of their number. While, normally, such trustees or executors may be entitled to act by a majority and quorum of their number, all letters of instructions or minutes should be signed by them all.

Cheques drawn on the account of a deceased customer are signed by his executors or, unless otherwise mentioned in the Confirmation in their favour, by a majority and quorum. The Confirmation should be produced to you before the cheques are paid, and, as the executors have no title to any assets of the deceased which are not included in the Confirmation, it is necessary to examine this document to see that the sum at the credit of the account has been properly included. If the amount at the credit of the account is more than the amount shown in the Confirmation, the executors have only a title to draw out the latter amount. To enable them to draw out the excess they require to expede and produce to you an Eik or additional Confirmation containing the amount of the excess.

Generally speaking, trustees and executors are not entitled to delegate their duties, and consequently if one of them has granted a power of attorney either in favour of one of his co-trustees or co-executors, or of some third person, you are not entitled to act upon it or accept the signature of such an attorney as coming in place of his principal as a trustee or executor.

Trustees are personally liable for cheques or bills drawn or indorsed by them in terms which do not expressly negative such liability. It is, of course, always a matter of construction of the particular documents as to whether the form of words used does or does not amount to such a negation.

Where trustees open an account in name of A. B. and C., the trustees of the late X., and the cheques are signed by the trustees, who may or may not add after their signature the words, " the trustees of the late X.," such trustees so signing are personally responsible. The addition to their signatures in this way must be regarded merely as descriptive. If care has been taken

26

at the time the account was opened to obtain a letter from the trustees or executors, such a question will not arise, as that letter, in the trustees' own interest, ought to negative their personal liability in case the account should become overdrawn.

An account in your books in name of " A. B. in trust for C. D." cannot be operated upon by C. D. as he is not your customer. He has, *ex facie*, however, the beneficial right to the sum at the credit and he may, therefore, intimate to you that you are not to pay any further cheques which A. B. may draw on the account, and you will be bound to give effect to this. The sum at credit can then only be drawn on the signatures of both, or by A. B. alone after C. D. has formally authorised you to that effect.

Apart from special circumstances, a trustee of this kind, while no doubt having authority to open and operate on a bank account, has no implied authority to overdraw it, and that being so, such trustee and not the principal would be responsible to the bank for any overdraft that might arise on the account.

The case of *The Royal Bank* v. *Skinner* (1931, S.L.T. 382) is interesting in this connection. In that case Mrs Cameron, a widow, carried on her husband's business after his death through a manager. Her law agent, Mr Skinner, arranged with the agent of the bank, who was conversant with the circumstances, for the opening of a current account. The account was entitled " J. M. Skinner for Mrs Duncan Cameron." An ordinary pass-book was kept by Mr Skinner, who drew on the account for the purposes of the business by cheques signed conform to the title of the account. After some years the business went wrong, there being an overdraft on the account which, having begun, had gone on increasing for a considerable period without objection by the bank or intimation by them to Mrs Cameron of its existence. Mrs Cameron ultimately granted a trust deed for behoof of her creditors, and the bank ranked on the trust estate for the overdraft and drew a dividend. Thereafter the bank sued Mr Skinner, the law agent, for the balance due, and the Court held that there was no accepted rule of law that a solicitor opening an account in his own name for a named client was personally responsible for the account, and that the authority to the law agent to open a credit account did not include authority to create a debit on the account ; but that, in this particular case, the overdraft must be regarded in a question with the bank as authorised by the client, in view of the bank having ranked therefor on Mrs Cameron's estate and drawn a dividend. The defender was accordingly assoilzied.

In that case, the bank, by ranking on Mrs Cameron's estate and claiming from Mr Skinner, were seeking to make both liable for the same debt, which, of course, was impossible. That was a case of an agent acting for a disclosed principal, and the law is that if the agent were duly authorised he personally is clear and the principal responsible. On the other hand, if the agent were not authorised, he alone is liable and the principal is clear. The bank by ranking on the principal's estate in this case had tacitly admitted that the agent was authorised, but they nevertheless tried to make him liable as if he had not been authorised—unsuccessfully, of course.

The authority of a mandatory or attorney to operate on his principal's bank account is limited

28

strictly by the powers conferred upon him by the terms of the document under which he acts. Unless it is expressed or clearly implied he has no right to operate on the account, still less has he any right to overdraw unless so authorised. In many cases you will find that an attorney is only authorised by his document to demand, sue for, uplift and recover all sums of money due to his principal without any reference being made to a bank account. Such a deed certainly authorises the attorney to draw out any sum there may be at the credit of the principal's account, but when he has done so his power as regards that asset is exhausted. You must not be misled by any general words appearing in the document, such as " to do all such other acts, and sign all such other documents as he may think necessary or desirable," as these words mean practically nothing. Nor is there any real meaning to you in a ratification clause in such a document whereby the principal agrees to ratify and confirm whatsoever the attorney may do or purport to do in virtue of his appointment.

The customer may be a firm, in which case cheques on the account will, in the absence of any special instructions, be validly drawn if signed in the firm name by any one of the partners, and this in terms of sec. 23 is equivalent to the signature by the partner so signing of the names of all persons liable as partners in that firm.

Each partner of a firm has implied authority to use the firm name and bind the firm in all matters relating to the partnership business, but that does not necessarily mean that he can commit the firm to an overdraft. It may or may not be within the requirements of the firm's business to borrow money. Take the case of professional

29

firms, where no trading is carried on, it is normally unnecessary to borrow money for the business, and in such a case it is outside the apparent scope of a partner's authority to incur an overdraft in the firm's name. It is, however, all a question of circumstances in each case, but you should keep the point prominently before you.

It is in accordance with the rules of good practice when you are asked to open an account in name of a firm to obtain a letter signed by all the partners requesting that the account be opened, giving specimen signatures, containing the instructions as to the method of operating on the account, authorising overdrafts, if and when sanctioned, by means of cheques signed by any one of the partners, and most important of all—and rarely attended to, by the way—providing for continuance in the event of the death of any of the partners.

While, generally speaking, any partner may draw cheques in the firm's name in connection with the partnership business, any of the other partners is entitled at any time to intimate to the bank that they are not to honour any more cheques so drawn, even although under the partnership agreement the drawing of cheques is specially committed to one particular partner alone. The bank are bound to act on such an intimation and stop operations on the account accordingly.

On any change in the constitution of a firm, whether by the death or retiral of one of the partners or the assumption of a new partner, that partnership is dissolved, and those continuing to carry on the business do so as a new and different firm even although the same firm name be used. Every known change in a partnership should, therefore, lead you to make enquiry as to what the arrangements are to be with regard to the continuation of the account, unless your covering letter is specific on this point.

This is a matter of great importance where the account is overdrawn, whether securities are held or not. The position, shortly stated, is that the estate of a deceased partner is not liable for any debts contracted by the firm after the date of his death, and when the old account is simply continued all payments lodged to its credit after the date of death go, in terms of Clayton's case (1 Mer. 529), to wipe out the debt outstanding at the date of death. Through operations being allowed on the account, therefore, although there may be no increase in the amount of the overdraft, the original debt and the liability therefor will be materially altered. The deceased partner's estate is relieved of responsibility, and any securities which may have been pledged for the old firm's debt will not be available for that of the new firm. This is well illustrated in the old case of *Christie* v. *The Royal Bank* (1841, 3 Ross's L.C. 668), where the bank in this way lost not only their claim against the deceased partner's estate but also the securities they held for the debt. If, therefore, you wish to retain the obligation of the deceased partner's estate and the securities held for the old firm's debt, you must close that account and thereby fix the liabilities as at that time. A new account should be opened in name of the new firm, even although carrying on business under the same name, and to this should be posted all receipts and payments subsequent to the death. The firm should be made aware that the old account has been closed and a new one opened, and a new pass-book should be issued.

In the case of a limited company customer,

it is obvious that it cannot deal with negotiable instruments otherwise than by delegated authority.

Such authority is to be found in the company's Memo. and Articles of Association and in the Minute by the directors prescribing the requirements suitable to their particular circumstances for signing and indorsing cheques.

A good deal of reliance can be placed on the authenticity of the certified excerpt Minute usually submitted to you in this case. If everything appears *ex facie* to be in order and in conformity with the Memo. and Articles of Association, you do not need to enquire whether it is so in fact. *Mahony* v. *The East Holyford Mining Co.* (L.R., 7 H.L. 869) is sufficient authority for that, but there may, of course, be circumstances where, from your own knowledge of the company's affairs, the position is quite different. *Liggett* v. *Barclays Bank* (1928, 1 K.B. 48) is a good example of a case of that kind, where an excerpt Minute was presented to the bank and acted on notwithstanding the fact they knew that, owing to the absence abroad of one of the only two directors, no such Minute could have been passed.

The terms of the excerpt Minute submitted to you by a limited company in this connection require your careful attention. For example, if the Minute authorises cheques to be signed on behalf of the company by any one of the directors and the secretary, and it so happens that one of the directors is also the secretary, it will not be within your authority to act on cheques signed only by that particular individual describing himself first as director and then as secretary, or describing himself merely as director and secretary. The obvious intention of such a Minute is that the cheques should be signed by two individuals and not by one only. Had it been otherwise, the Minute would simply have authorised cheques to be signed by any one of the directors. It is not only the words used that require consideration in each case, but also, and equally important, the implication of these words.

As regards the termination of the authority of a director to sign cheques on behalf of a company, this may take place through his having resigned office or becoming bankrupt, or being removed from office by the shareholders and so on, but so long as you have no actual knowledge of his appointment being terminated you are at liberty to honour the company's cheques bearing his signature. It is for the company to keep you advised of the changes which take place.

Company cheques, however, are sometimes presented for payment bearing the signature of a director who may have died or resigned, or been otherwise removed from office after such cheques had been issued. If you are satisfied that these cheques were issued before the appointment terminated, then you are in safety to pay them because the signature is the signature of the company. In the ordinary case a cheque signed by a mandatory or attorney cannot be paid after the death of the principal, but such a cheque may be paid notwithstanding the subsequent death of the mandatory or attorney. It is this latter position which arises on the death or resignation of a director of a company.

As regards the termination of the authority of the whole directors in connection with the drawing of cheques preceding a liquidation, the position is that in the case of a winding-up by the Court the directors' powers cease on the presentation of the petition for liquidation, which is, of course, advertised. In the case of a voluntary winding-up, the directors' powers do not come to an end on the calling of the meeting, but only on the actual passing by the shareholders of the resolution that the company should be wound up.

With regard to the possible question not infrequently raised as to whether a limited company is liable on a bill or cheque, or whether the directors signing it are personally liable instead, the rule is that, if it appears on the face of the document that in terms of the Companies Acts the directors sign only for and on behalf of the company, they are not personally liable.

In *Chapman* v. *Smethurst* (1909, 1 K.B. 927) a promissory note, beginning " I promise to pay," was signed by the managing director of a company, the name of the company being stamped above the signature and the words " Managing Director " below. The Court held that the document had been properly signed on behalf of the company and that they were liable thereon.

If, on the other hand, directors sign a cheque or bill merely describing themselves as directors and not expressing that they are acting for and on behalf of the company, they are personally liable. The case of *Brebner* v. *Henderson* (1925, S.C. 643) is a good example of such a position. A promissory note had been granted in the following terms :—

Four months after date we promise to pay to A.B. within the office of the X Bank the sum of £175 Stg. Value received.

> C.D., *Director.*
> E.F., *Secretary.*
> The Fraserburgh Empire Ltd.

The Court held that the director and secretary who had signed this note were personally liable for its amount, in respect that they had failed to show either that the words appended to their signatures were more than descriptive or that they indicated that the signatures were appended " for and on behalf of " the company in the sense of sec. 26 of the 1882 Act, or that the note had been made " by or on behalf or on account of the company " in the sense of sec. 77 of the Companies Act of 1908, which is similar in terms to sec. 30 of the 1929 Act. A somewhat similar case is that of *M'Meekin* v. *Easton* (1889, 16 R. 363) relating to a promissory note granted by three individuals in the name and on behalf of the Reformed Presbyterian Church, Stranraer, but who were found personally liable for the amount of the note.

Where a question of liability is raised as indicated in these cases as between a company on the one hand and the signing directors on the other, you will keep in view that, as in Skinner's case, you cannot have both as your obligants, so that, if the directors are personally liable, the company are not—and *vice versa*.

LECTURE II.

WITH the view of ensuring that payment of the sum contained in a cheque is duly received by the person intended, the drawer of the cheque may so arrange that it is not to be transferable or payable to any other person, or that it can only be transferred under certain limitations, or that it can only be paid in some particular way.

Under sec. 60 it is provided that when a cheque payable to order is paid in good faith and in the ordinary course of business by the banker on whom it is drawn, it is not incumbent on that banker to show that the indorsement of the payee or any subsequent indorsement was made by or under the authority of the person whose indorsement it purports to be, and the banker is deemed to have paid the cheque in due course, although such indorsement has been forged or made without authority. Sec. 19 of the 1853 Act is in similar terms, but does not contain the qualification as to payment in good faith and in the ordinary course of business.

If, therefore, a banker in good faith and in the ordinary course of business happens to pay a cheque or draft made payable to order on which the payee's indorsement has been forged, he is entitled to debit the amount to the drawer's account, and it is then a question for the drawer

37

and payee to settle between themselves as to who should bear the loss. That, naturally, will depend on the circumstances and also on whether either was guilty of negligence or of failure in duty to the other.

If such a cheque, however, is not made payable to order, the paying banker's position is not protected by either the 1853 Act or the 1882 Act, and care requires to be taken to obviate running inadvertently into liability to the drawer because of a forged indorsement. Under sec. 8 of the 1882 Act a cheque payable to A. without the addition of the words " or order " is nevertheless payable to his order, and is accordingly within sec. 60, but a cheque payable to " A. only," or marked " not transferable," or bearing other words prohibiting transfer or indicating an intention that it should not be transferable, is not within the protection afforded by sec. 60, and, in such a case, the paying banker is responsible for seeing that payment is made to the correct payee and to no one else.

Sections 76 to 82, which are usually referred to as the " Crossed Cheque Sections," enable the drawer or the holder to put a crossing on the cheque which may be either general or special, and he may add the words " not negotiable." The essential part of a crossing is two parallel transverse lines, and these are sufficient without the addition of " & Co." or any other words. Shortly stated, the effect of a general crossing is to give instructions to the paying banker that the cheque is to be paid only to a banker, and, in the case of a special crossing, only to the banker whose name has been written across the face of the cheque. If the paying banker ignores the instruction given to him by any such crossing or acts in contravention of it he is liable to the true owner of the cheque for any loss he may sustain owing to the cheque having been so paid. Protection, however, is given to the paying banker by sec. 80 in every case where in good faith and without negligence he pays a cheque, crossed generally to a banker, or, if crossed specially, to the banker to whom it is so crossed.

There is nothing to prevent a paying banker cashing a crossed cheque over the counter if he is satisfied that he is paying the money to the actual payee of the cheque, but, if he should happen to be mistaken as to the identity of the person cashing the cheque and loss occurs thereby, he will be responsible therefor because of his having disregarded the instruction contained in the crossing.

So far as concerns a collecting banker who is asked to cash or collect an uncrossed cheque drawn on another banker, he is not protected under sec. 60 because that section relates only to the paying banker—*i.e.*, the banker on whom the cheque is drawn—but, as a collecting banker, he is protected in the case of a crossed cheque under sec. 82 if, in good faith and without negligence, he receives from the paying banker payment for a customer of a crossed cheque even although such customer has no title or a defective title thereto.

Such collection, however, must be for a customer, and a customer, generally speaking, is a person who has a current account and not merely one dealing only in deposit receipts or exchanging cheques for cash. If, therefore, as a collecting banker, you collect or pay cash for a crossed cheque to someone who is not a current account customer, you are not protected by sec. 82 and may be liable for the amount to the true owner.

Shortly stated, therefore, the position of the collecting banker as regards forged indorsements is that if anything is wrong he is responsible therefor where he cashes or collects a crossed cheque for someone who has no current account, and also in all cases where he cashes an uncrossed cheque drawn on another banker.

The theory on which a collecting banker is liable for a forged indorsement on an uncrossed cheque appears to be that his intervention in the matter is purely voluntary, and as a matter of convenience for his customer, to whom alone he should look for protection. In the case of a crossed cheque, however, the drawer has specially directed his own banker—the paying banker— to pay it only through a banker, which, of necessity, involves the intervention of the collecting banker to carry out the drawer's instructions and, because of that, the collecting banker is given immunity in the case of such crossed cheques.

Under sec. 77 the holder of an uncrossed cheque may cross it either generally or specially, and where an uncrossed cheque is sent to a banker for collection he may cross it specially to himself. While, therefore, a collecting banker has protection in the case of a crossed cheque, but has no protection in the case of an uncrossed cheque, it might be supposed that this section would enable him as holder to cross it himself and so bring himself within the protection afforded by sec. 82. That, however, is not the case, because what he really is collecting, so far as his customer is concerned, is an uncrossed cheque.

The words " not negotiable " appearing on the face of a cheque as part of the crossing do not mean that it is not to be negotiated or transferred, but merely that, in terms of sec. 81, the person taking such a cheque does not obtain and cannot give to a subsequent indorsee any better title to it than that which the person from whom he took it had. An indorsee of such a cheque does not obtain any worse title. In fact, he acquires all that his indorser had—no more, but, on the other hand, no less.

Consequently no one can become a holder in due course of such a cheque, as the object of the addition to the crossing of the words " not negotiable " is to give protection to the true owner of the cheque by preserving his right against any subsequent holder. If the cheque is dishonoured or stopped, the indorsee, if he is the true owner of the cheque, has the same rights against the drawer as he would have had on an open cheque. If the drawer refuses to recognise liability to the holder of such a cheque it is for him to prove the defect in title—not for the holder to prove that there is no defect.

Although a doubt on the point has been suggested, it is clear that the words " not negotiable " appearing as part of a crossing have no prejudicial effect upon the immunity of the collecting banker under sec. 82. That section says distinctly that the collecting banker who receives payment is protected although his customer has no title or a defective title. In this way he may be in a better position than his customer.

If, however, the collecting banker has not yet actually received payment of such a crossed cheque, but has it returned through the clearing unpaid for some reason or other, he is not in that case in any better position than his customer, as neither he nor anyone else can be a holder in due course of such a cheque. He, therefore, requires in these circumstances to rely upon the validity of every indorsement on the cheque, and, if any of the indorsements be forged, he has no title to the cheque. All he can do is to look to his own customer for relief, and rely upon his indorsement.

If the words " not negotiable " appear by themselves on a cheque without the parallel transverse lines referred to in sec. 76 they do not make that cheque a crossed cheque within the meaning of the Act. Consequently there is no protection to the banker under sec. 80 or sec. 82. Indeed it is questionable whether even the paying banker in such a case is protected under sec. 60, which you will recollect relates only to the payment of a cheque payable to order, as it may be possible to say that a cheque like this is not payable to order.

There are three classes of cheques contemplated by the Act, and you will find them dealt with in sec. 8. They are as follows :—

1. Cheques which contain words prohibiting transfer or indicating an intention that they should not be transferable. These are referred to as not negotiable cheques.
2. Negotiable cheques payable to order.
3. Negotiable cheques payable to bearer.

In *Hibernian Bank Ltd.* v. *Gysin and Hanson* (54 T.L.R. 780) it was held that a bill of exchange payable to " the order of —— only " and crossed " not negotiable " was not negotiable, and the contention that a bill payable to order can never be not negotiable could not be upheld. This upsets the dicta of Lord Justices Lindley, Bowen and Fry in *National Bank* v. *Silke* (1891, 1 K.B. 437), where they laid down that a bill cannot be made not negotiable under sec. 8.

If a cheque is marked " not negotiable " without

parallel transverse lines, and is expressed to be payable to the payee without the addition of the words " or order," the inference would appear to be that it is not a transferable cheque and is not payable to order as contemplated by sec. 60.

On the other hand, if a cheque is marked " not negotiable " without parallel transverse lines, but contains the words " to order," the paying banker cannot insist upon its being presented through a banker as a crossed cheque and he would incur no liability under sec. 79 if he paid over the counter. It is really an uncrossed cheque and bears to be payable to order so that he would be protected under sec. 60.

If, however, such a cheque when presented for payment bears evidence of having been negotiated, the paying banker may either pay it or refuse payment. He could justify his paying it on the ground that the words " not negotiable " had no meaning when the words " or order " also appeared on the face of the cheque, and he could likewise justify a refusal to pay on the ground that the cheque was contradictory, embarrassing and irregular. You will, of course, appreciate that it is inconsistent to make a cheque payable to order and at the same time put on it a marking of some kind to prevent it from being transferred or negotiated.

As a further precaution against loss the drawer may write the words " Account Payee " or " Account Payee only " across the face of the cheque as part of the crossing. These words are not authorised by the Act, and, while they have been under judicial consideration in several cases, their full import and effect cannot be laid down in detail. They probably do not affect the transferability of the cheque particularly when the words " or order " appear immediately after the payee's name. If the words " or order " are absent the cheque would probably fall to be regarded as not transferable. There can be little doubt that a banker paying cash for such a cheque or crediting it to an account not in name of the payee does so at his own risk. It is, therefore, necessary for you to be satisfied as to how the cheque comes to be in the hands of a holder who is not lodging it to the credit of the payee's account.

As you will see from these remarks there is a lack of appreciation on the part of the drawer, and I am afraid also on the part of bankers, of the inconsistency of making a cheque payable to order and at the same time marking it " not transferable " or "Account Payee only " or even " not negotiable " without parallel transverse lines. In effect, the result is that the cheque is neither clearly negotiable nor clearly not negotiable.

If he makes out his cheque consistently and makes it payable to A. only, or otherwise indicates an intention that it is not to be transferred, the customer protects himself and the payee absolutely without the necessity even of using a crossing, and he puts upon the collecting and the paying bankers the whole responsibility for the safety of the money. In theory, a cheque is simply a mandate by the customer to his banker to pay a certain sum to A., and if the banker, as he has presumably undertaken, is to carry out the mandate he must justify what he does or take refuge in some exemption either under the Act or under a special contract. There is, however, no exemption given under any of the Acts in respect of a non-transferable cheque, and the only alternative is for the banker to contract out of responsibility therefor.

A cheque requires to be presented for payment, and this should be done within a reasonable time of its issue. As between the drawer and payee the question of what is a reasonable time does not usually arise, because the cheque only operates payment of a debt subject to the resolutive condition that it be honoured, and the payee is entitled to ask payment of the cheque from the drawer at any time within six years. The only exception to this is where in the meantime the banker, on whom the cheque is drawn and who had funds available to meet the cheque, fails before it is presented for payment. Under sec. 74 the drawer of such a cheque is discharged, and the payee is penalised for his delay in being limited to a ranking on the banker's estate for the amount of the cheque. The same position holds good in a question between the drawer and an indorsee.

As between the payee and his indorsee and as between the collecting banker and his customer the presentment for payment must be made within a reasonable time, which is determined by the circumstances, but may generally be taken as allowing for presentment the day after receipt and where an agent intervenes in the collection the day after receipt by him.

It is the duty of the banker on whom a cheque is drawn to make payment thereof, provided it is in order and he has funds in hand or has otherwise arranged with the drawer to meet it. If in any particular case you consider it necessary to refuse payment of a cheque, you must make sure that you give the correct reason for doing so. If you have more reasons than one you should state them all at the time, and not merely only one of them, because of the legal results of presentment to which I shall refer shortly. For example—

payment may be refused in a single case on account
of insufficient funds, payment stopped, indorsement irregular, words and figures differ and so
on. It may be that any one of these reasons is
quite good enough for not paying that particular
cheque, but, if you state only one of them, you
may mislead the payee and involve yourself in
complications. Further, you must be tactful and
must not say anything which might prejudicially
affect your customer's credit. For instance, if
your customer's balance has been arrested by a
creditor, you must not say so to the payee of one
of his cheques, payment of which you refuse because
of that. The answer in such a case is—Refer to
drawer.

In order to enable a banker to pay a cheque
drawn on him, the document, unless payable to
bearer, requires to be indorsed by the payee.
If payable to bearer indorsement is not required,
but you will keep in mind the remarks I made
in the previous lecture as to the desirability of
having bearer cheques indorsed.

The cheque must be properly indorsed—that is,
it must be indorsed or purport to be indorsed
by or under the authority of the payee and, if
not so indorsed, payment should be refused as
the drawer may justifiably decline to allow the
cheque to be debited to his account.

I do not propose to deal with the many and
varied questions of what is and what is not a
proper indorsement, and it will, I think, be sufficient for the present purpose if you will keep in
mind the general rule just mentioned—that is,
that the cheque must be indorsed or purport to
be indorsed by or under the authority of the
payee.

I should, however, draw your attention to

Slingsby v. *The District Bank* (1932, 1 K.B. 544), where a cheque which read as having been made payable to John Prust & Co. per Cumberbirch & Potts was paid on the simple indorsement " Cumberbirch & Potts " without any reference to the payees, John Prust & Co. The Court of Appeal held that such an indorsement was irregular and invalid and that the paying bank were negligent in honouring the cheque, and for that reason, of course, were not protected either by sec. 60 or sec. 80.

While in accordance with Scots Law, a document being executed by some person who cannot write requires to be executed on his behalf by a solicitor, notary public or justice of the peace, the practice with regard to the indorsement by a payee who cannot write is to have the payee put his mark in the form of a X on the back of the cheque in presence of one witness who writes the payee's name and then signs his own name and adds his address and occupation. Some think that as most documents in Scotland require two witnesses, there should be two witnesses in the case of such an indorsement, but I hardly think that that is really necessary. The Act makes no express provision for such a case, but it allows any signature to be adhibited by some other person if so done by or under the authority of the party whose signature is required. In this way, all that is necessary for you to do is to preserve evidence that such authority has been duly given, and the evidence of one witness is probably quite sufficient for that purpose. You will, of course, be careful in a case of this kind to act with proper caution so that a charge of negligence may not be made against you.

As regards the formal indorsement of cheques,

particularly of those which are lodged to the
credit of the payee's account, an enormous amount
of work is involved each day not only on the
part of the payees themselves but also on the
part of collecting bankers all over the country
who are called upon to guarantee indorsements
made on behalf of certain customers by their
cashiers or other employees.

In my own office where the work of indorsement
is not left to the cashier, it is aggravating, particularly at term times, to have to spend time
which could be employed to better advantage
in what we facetiously refer to as " practising
handwriting."   It is unfair to expect a banker
to do gratuitously what is obviously a vast amount
of work of supererogation—that is, guaranteeing
the indorsements put on by the cashiers or other
employees of customers who more or less selfishly
think rather of their own time than they do of
their bankers'.

It should not be a difficult matter and would be
to the great advantage not only of the customer,
but also of his banker, if some general arrangement
could be come to whereby cheques lodged to the
credit of the payee's account should not require
indorsement, but should be deemed to be sufficiently indorsed for all purposes if impressed with
a stamp of some kind indicating that the payee's
account had been credited with the amount.   In
one or two cases here and there a special arrangement on something like these lines is in force and
works quite well and saves a considerable amount
of time and trouble, and there seems to be no good
reason why a general arrangement should not be
made along these lines with, at any rate, a large
proportion of every banker's customers.

One of the reasons sometimes given for the

non-payment of a cheque is that payment has been countermanded by the drawer. To be effectual the countermand must, of course, be received before the cheque is actually paid. So far as the paying banker is concerned, he must obey his customer's instructions, provided they be clear and definite. Such instructions should be in writing, and, if your customer has merely telephoned or telegraphed to you to stop payment, you should ask him to write you confirming, and at the same time write him yourself recording the instructions.

So far as the collecting banker is concerned he requires to consider his own position in the case of a stopped cheque. There is no obligation on him to take any steps in the matter beyond informing his customer of what has happened and debiting back to him the amount of the cheque. If the customer's position is satisfactory all is well, but if it is not then the collecting banker will naturally endeavour to enforce payment of the cheque in his own interests.

Any holder for value, including a collecting banker, whether his customer's account is overdrawn or not, is entitled to enforce payment of a stopped cheque. The paying banker is, of course, under no liability on such a cheque, but the drawer is and he may be sued in the usual way. The indorsers are also liable under sec. 55 and may also be sued, but, so far as they are concerned, notice of the dishonour should be given to them in accordance with sec. 49. No notice requires to be given to the drawer as sec. 50 excuses the necessity for notice being given to him in a case of this kind.

When a cheque is lost the drawer should not merely, on countermanding payment, issue a new cheque in its place, but should also obtain a security or indemnity from the payee as contemplated under sec. 69. It may quite well be that the lost cheque may ultimately find its way into the hands of a holder in due course to whom the countermand of payment is no answer, thus possibly involving the drawer in double payment of the amount. It may be a nice question between the drawer and the original payee in a case of this kind as to which of them should bear the loss and as to whether the extra payment under either the first or the second cheque was made under a mistake in fact or a mistake in law.

It is expected on the part of every customer that the bank, in dealing with his affairs, will do so in the ordinary course of business, and that nothing will be done out of the usual routine. For example, a customer is entitled to rely upon your confining your activities as regards payment of his cheques to the usual banking hours, and that if he wishes to stop payment of any cheque which he has issued he has the whole period from three o'clock on one day to ten o'clock the following morning to give the necessary instructions. You should, therefore, not pay any cheques outside of the usual hours, otherwise you may find you have paid one which your customer in quite good time tells you not to pay, and in such a case the loss will be yours. In *Baines* v. *The National Provincial Bank* (1927, 37 T.L.R. 631), where a cheque was presented and paid at five minutes past three o'clock, and instructions to stop payment were received by the bank before the opening hour next day, the Court held that the bank were entitled to a reasonable business margin to deal with a cheque presented to them for payment. The drawer in that case had issued the cheque

50

just before three o'clock, thinking that it could not be presented and paid that day, and with the deliberate intention of countermanding payment in good time before the bank opened the following morning. He was, however, prevented from doing so because the bank had paid the cheque after hours on the day of issue.

Do not, however, rely upon Baines' case to any great extent, but rather endeavour to confine the payment of cheques strictly to the recognised business hours. In particular, do not rely upon Baines' case at all if you must refuse payment of a cheque for any reason. For example, if you have no funds in hand to meet a cheque presented to you for payment a minute or so after three o'clock your customer may, like Baines, have had the intention of lodging money to his credit before the cheque could normally be presented for payment, but by your refusing payment after business hours you may have damaged his credit.

When a cheque is presented to a paying banker, it operates, in terms of sec. 53, as a formal intimation to him of an assignation by the drawer of the cheque in favour of the payee or indorsee of the funds belonging to the drawer in the hands of the banker to the extent of the sum in the cheque. If the sum at the credit is sufficient to meet the cheque no question arises and payment is made accordingly, assuming that the cheque is in order, but, if the sum at credit is insufficient, the position is otherwise. In this there is an important difference between the law of England and the law of Scotland, and it is necessary for you to have the point continually before you.

If there is a sum at the credit of your customer's account, or on a balance of all his accounts if he has more than one, but it is insufficient to meet

51

in full the cheque presented to you, you require to transfer the sum at the credit of the account or the net balance at the credit of all the accounts, as the case may be, to the credit of a separate account, specially earmarking it as against the cheque so presented. The cheque is then returned to the holder with the answer " insufficient funds." If payment of a cheque has been countermanded by the drawer before it is presented, you should likewise on the presentment of the cheque transfer the amount to a separate account earmarked as just mentioned. In that case, the answer will be " payment stopped," and if the funds were insufficient to meet the cheque in full you should add " insufficient funds " so as to disclose the real position.

The holder of a cheque of which payment is refused on account of there being insufficient funds to meet it, is entitled to know how much has been attached by the presentment, and, if he asks, you are bound to tell him. He is entitled and may be willing to take payment of the amount so attached, in which case he will deliver up the cheque to you with a receipt endorsed thereon for the amount so paid to him. If he is unwilling to follow this course, payment of the sum attached and transferred as above-mentioned can thereafter only be made by you with the consent of both parties, and if no agreement is reached between them, the matter is usually settled in Court in the form of an action of multiplepoinding.

In this connection it is desirable for you to have your books written up as far as possible as you go along, because you may otherwise inadvertently get into confusion where several cheques are presented to you within a few minutes of each other. The cheque which is presented to you first in point of time is entitled to preference, and the funds should be transferred and earmarked for that cheque—those subsequently presented being returned with the answer " refer to drawer."

Where several cheques are presented to you through the one clearing or by the same post, they are all entitled to rank *pari passu*. Transfer of the funds should also be made in such a case and earmarked for all these cheques, which should be returned with the answer " refer to drawer." You should not give the answer " insufficient funds " on these cheques, because that answer on any one of them may be untrue. You may have sufficient in hand to meet one of them although insufficient to meet them all.

The assignment effected by the presentment of a cheque applies, of course, only where there is a credit balance at the actual time of the presentment and does not affect sums subsequently lodged to the credit of the account. It has not been decided whether the presentment of a cheque, where there are insufficient or no funds at the credit of the account, has any effect in attaching sums at the credit of the drawer which are on deposit receipt, or on deposit or savings account or bills, &c., lodged for collection, but while the presented cheque is primarily intended to form a charge on a current account, there does not appear to be any good reason in law why it should not have the effect of attaching these other items, if any. What the Act states as attached by such presentment are funds in the hands of the drawee available for the payment thereof, which seems wide enough, at any rate, to cover deposit receipts and savings accounts. Pending any decision on the point, it would be well for you to proceed on the footing that such deposits and savings are so

53

attached, as otherwise your customer might have a serious complaint against you for dishonouring one of his cheques while you had plenty of his money to meet it. The payee would, in such a case, receive an entirely untrue impression of the drawer's financial position.

The question is sometimes raised as to whether attachment of funds is legally effected by the presentment of a cheque which is not properly indorsed, or, it may be, not indorsed at all, or it may even be a post-dated cheque. The answer lies in the terms of sec. 53 (2), which says that the bill—or cheque—operates as an assignment of the sum for which it is drawn in favour of the holder from the time when the bill—or cheque —is presented to the drawee. You will notice that it is the bill or cheque itself which operates as the assignment and not its presentment—the presentment is only the time when the assignment takes effect in your hands.

Apart from sec. 53, however, it appears to be the common law of Scotland that a cheque operates as an assignation. In *The British Linen Bank* v. *Carruthers* (1883, 10 R. 923), Lord Shand said on this subject :—

" The statute enacts the common law of Scotland that a cheque or a bill of exchange, when intimated, is effectual as an intimated assignation. It appears to me that the statute only carries out what it is understood was intended —a consolidation of the existing Scotch Law. There is nothing new in it. I agree that a cheque granted for onerous causes to a third party according to the common law is, on being intimated, equivalent to an assignation."

Sec. 53, you will notice, does not say presentment for payment, it simply says presented to the drawee. In any case, sec. 45, which prescribes the circumstances under which a bill or cheque is duly presented for payment, does not make any reference to the necessity or otherwise of an indorsement.

The correct position, therefore, appears to be that a cheque is the equivalent of an assignation and, to complete the assignee's right, intimation requires to be given. Such intimation may apparently even be given notarially in the usual way without actual presentment so that the absence or invalidity of an indorsement is of no importance.

In these circumstances, when you find it necessary to return a cheque because it has not been properly indorsed, you should regard its presentation as having the effect of an intimated assignation, and make the necessary transfer of funds in your books.

In this connection, it is interesting to refer to the case of a cheque, payment of which is guaranteed by the paying bank before the customer delivers it to the payee in settlement of some transaction between them. The exact effect of such a guarantee has not been legally decided, but no doubt the Court would hold the bank liable to pay the amount in the cheque in accordance with the wording of their guarantee. Apart from that, however, the fact that such a cheque has been presented unindorsed to the paying bank may, in Scotland, have the effect of intimating an assignment of the amount contained in it, notwithstanding that delivery to the payee has not yet been made.

Under sec. 9, where the sum in a cheque is expressed in words, and also in figures, and there is a discrepancy between the two, the sum denoted by the words is the amount payable. The practice, as you know, however, is to return such a cheque

with the answer " words and figures differ,"
notwithstanding that the indorsement is all in
order and to ignore such presentment as having
the effect of an intimated assignation. This, I
think, is wrong, because the words of the section
are quite clear, and the payee or indorsee would
appear to have right to enforce payment of the
amount denoted by the words in the cheque.
If, however, for your own protection, you think
it well to return such a cheque with the answer
referred to, you should take the further step of
transferring the amount denoted by the words
to a separate account earmarked to meet that
particular cheque.

If the amount denoted by the words of such a
cheque is greater than the amount in figures, your
position in transferring the larger amount to the
separate account is secure. But, if it should happen
that the amount in figures is greater than the
amount denoted by the words, you will not be
in safety to transfer the larger amount as that
is not what the Act says is the amount payable.
If you transfer the larger amount denoted by the
figures you may thereby unnecessarily deplete
your customer's balance to such an extent that
a cheque subsequently presented is returned by
you marked " insufficient funds." In these circumstances you may be liable in damages to your
customer.

On the reasoning above indicated, the presentment of a post-dated cheque before its due date
operates as an intimation of a completed assignation to the same effect as if the presentment had
been made on or after the due date. In this
respect a post-dated cheque is similar to a Bill
of Exchange drawn at a currency presented to
the drawee for acceptance even although the

date of payment may be some time in the future. A transfer of funds should also be made in a case of this kind.

As we shall see later, when an arrestment has been lodged in your hands attaching your customer's balance, you require to make provision therefor to enable you to implement the Decree of Furthcoming which, sooner or later, the arresting creditor will probably produce.

It not infrequently happens that arrestments are used by a creditor to an undue extent, in which case they may be recalled by the Court. It also happens sometimes that the arresting creditor and his debtor arrange matters between themselves, when the arresting creditor or his solicitor will hand over to his debtor a letter addressed to you withdrawing the arrestment. In some cases also an arrestment may be ineffectual for some technical reason or another.

In these circumstances, if a cheque or a series of cheques is presented to you for payment after your customer's balance has been arrested, it is necessary for you to take care, in the event of the arrestment being later on for any reason recalled, withdrawn or cancelled, and the customer's balance accordingly still left in your hands, that you have made the necessary provision for paying the cheques in question in the due order in which they have been presented to you. Each cheque takes priority according to the time of its presentment to you, and you should therefore in the circumstances outlined above keep an exact record of the cheques so presented to you following upon an arrestment, and of the order in which they are so presented, and, after the withdrawal or cancellation of the arrestment, make payment in accordance with that order so far as your customer's balance will go. If this is not attended to, you will appreciate that trouble may arise owing possibly to your having paid away your customer's balance in satisfying a cheque which was not the first presented to you after the arrestment.

The theory underlying this position is that the presentment of a cheque operates as an assignation of the funds as they existed in your hands at the time subject to any lien or counterclaim which you yourselves might have, and subject to claims on the part of others such as those of an arresting creditor. If these incumbrances, as they may be termed, fly off, the funds are left free in your hands to meet the claims of effective assignations in the form of cheques presented to you in their due order of presentment.

As I previously mentioned, a countermand of payment requires, in order to be effectual, to be given prior to payment being actually made, although it may be given after the cheque has been presented. In such a case payment cannot be made, but if there are funds in hand, the presentment operates, as I have explained, as an intimated assignation.

One or two illustrations of this position may be helpful to you. For example, a cheque drawn on you by one of your customers who has funds at his credit sufficient to meet it, is received by you through the clearing having been negotiated through a banker in a provincial town. At, say, 2 P.M. that day you receive instructions from your customer to stop payment. The question at once arises as to whether the cheque has been paid before you received the countermand, in which case the matter is closed and nothing can be done, or whether the countermand has been

58

received after presentment but before payment is made, in which case the presentment operates as an intimated assignation and the cheque should be returned with the answer " payment stopped."

To determine the question as to whether the countermand has been received before or after payment, we require to consider what steps are actually taken by the paying banker following upon the presentment of the cheque. If he has funds in hand, he will, as soon as he can in the ordinary course of business, make the necessary entries in the cash book and following upon that in the ledger. In my view, the entries in the cash book, immediately on being made, constitute payment and create a new legal position. If the countermand of payment is received after the cash book entries are put through, you are not justified in deleting them and thereby making another alteration in the legal position.

If, however, there are no funds in hand to meet a cheque so presented to you through the clearing, you will naturally retain the cheque until the close of business, because your customer may by that time lodge money to the credit of his account to enable you to meet the cheque. When that has been done, you will, of course, proceed to put the necessary entries relating to the cheque through your cash book at which point of time payment is deemed to have been made.

A somewhat similar position arises where your customer lodges for the credit of his account a cheque drawn in his favour by another of your customers at the same branch. Almost immediately after the cheque has been paid in and entered in the payee's pass book, but before it is debited to the drawer's account in your ledger, the drawer

59

himself calls and countermands payment. Such a countermand comes too late, because the payee has had his pass book initialled in respect of the credit to his account, and that to him is the equivalent of the receipt of the money itself. It is of no importance that the credit entry has not yet reached the payee's account in your ledger, or that the debit entry has not yet been made in the drawer's account.

Questions as to indorsement of cheques and the treatment of cheques lodged for collection, and the negligence of bankers connected therewith, have been dealt with in a series of cases of importance to you, and as the decisions are not altogether in accordance with what has hitherto been regarded as quite good practice, it is necessary that they should receive your serious consideration.

The first case to which I would direct your attention in this connection is that of *Underwood Ltd.* v. *The Bank of Liverpool & Martins* (1924, 1 K.B. 775). This was an instance of a one man company. That one man was the sole director, and he indorsed certain of the company's cheques and paid them to the credit of his own private bank account. The Court held that that constituted a conversion of the ownership of the cheques, because the bank were not entitled to collect the proceeds of these cheques and to appropriate them to the personal account of the sole director, and, that being so, the bank had misapplied the company's property and so were liable for conversion.

As a contrast to that case, you may have a firm with only one partner. If he indorses a cheque drawn in favour of his firm and pays it, not into the firm's account, but into his own personal account, no harm is done and you run no risk.

The reason is that, as sole partner of the firm, he is personally responsible for all the firm's debts, and it does not matter whether he keeps the firm's money in one pocket or the other. The sole director of a limited company is in an entirely different position, as he is not liable for the company's debts, so that the company's creditors are entitled to expect that the company's money will not be mixed up with the private money of the director. The same applies to the case of a firm where there is more than one partner, so that before crediting any firm's cheque to the private account of a partner, you must be quite sure that he is the sole partner, otherwise his co-partner may have something to say to you.

The next case of this kind worthy of note is that of *The Midland Bank* v. *Reckitt* (1933, A.C. 1). In that case Lord Terrington, who was the attorney for Sir Harold Reckitt, and had unlimited power to draw cheques on his principal's account, was himself personally indebted to the Midland Bank on two overdraft accounts in name of his firm, who were the solicitors for Sir Harold Reckitt. Terrington was pressed from time to time by the Midland Bank to put his accounts in order, and on each occasion he, as attorney for Sir Harold Reckitt, drew cheques on his principal's account with Barclay's Bank and paid the amounts to the credit of his firm's accounts with the Midland Bank. The Midland Bank accepted these cheques without question, although it was fairly obvious that the money they were getting did not belong to their customer. When Terrington's defalcations were discovered, Sir Harold Reckitt sued the Midland Bank as the collecting bankers for the sums represented by the cheques in question on the ground of conversion and negligence, and the Court of Appeal had little difficulty in deciding against the bank.

This case and that of Underwood, which I have just mentioned, bear out the well-known maxim that what goes in to the credit of an account requires on the banker's part just as much careful scrutiny as that which goes out, and you should always keep this in mind.

I have referred already on more than one occasion to the Slingsby cases, which are also of great importance to you. Slingsby and others were the executors of the late Harry Turner, and kept an account in their own name with the District Bank at Macclesfield. Their solicitors were Cumberbirch & Potts, who kept their account with the Westminster Bank at Manchester, while Cumberbirch himself kept his personal account with the same bank at Macclesfield.

Cumberbirch carried on a series of frauds for a time without being discovered, but when the real position was ascertained Slingsby found that the executors had sustained serious losses through the actings of Cumberbirch.

The executors first raised an action against the Westminster Bank as the collecting bankers for conversion of the sum contained in a dividend warrant in respect of War Stock which they held. This warrant had been signed by Slingsby as the first named executor and handed to Cumberbirch to be credited to the executor's account. Instead of doing so he paid it into his own private account with the Westminster Bank, who were apparently satisfied with the explanation which Cumberbirch gave them as to the ownership of the dividend warrant (1931, 1 K.B. 173).

Finlay, J., who tried the case in the first instance,

held that a warrant for payment of dividend on War Stock was a crossed cheque within the meaning of the Act, and this point may now be taken as settled. He also held that the Westminster Bank had acted in good faith and without negligence, and that they were protected by sec. 82 and therefore not liable. Although this case was not appealed, the latter part of his decision was disapproved by the Court of Appeal in the District Bank case to which I shall refer in a moment.

The next action which the executors raised against the Westminster Bank as the collecting bankers was for conversion of a sum of £5000 contained in the cheque which I have already mentioned to you, first as having had an addition made to the payee's name and second as having been improperly indorsed (1931, 2 K.B. 583).

Finlay, J., who also tried this case, again absolved the bank from negligence and held that there had been no conversion. This case was not appealed either, but the decision was disapproved in the succeeding case.

The executors who had been unsuccessful down to this point then made a claim against their own bankers, the District Bank, for the £5000 in question (1932, 1 K.B. 544). Wright, J., who tried the case, having found in favour of the executors, the bank appealed—unsuccessfully, however. The Court of Appeal held—as regards the points in the case which affect the present subject—(1) that the cheque had been materially altered within the meaning of sec. 64 and was therefore void as between the bank and their customers ; (2) that therefore the bank could not rely upon sec. 60 or upon sec. 80 ; (3) that the indorsement of Cumberbirch & Potts alone without any reference to the name of the payees, John Prust & Co., was irregular and invalid ; (4) that the bank were negligent in honouring the cheque and so not protected by the Act ; and (5) that the drawers had not been negligent in leaving a blank space between the payees' name and the printed words " or order."

The next case is that of *Lloyds Bank* v. *Savory* (1933, A.C. 201). There Savory & Co., a firm of stockbrokers in London, were in the habit of signing cheques drawn on their account with the Midland Bank, which were intended to be applied in payment of jobbers' accounts, and which in accordance with a rule of the London Stock Exchange were crossed and made payable to bearer.

These brokers had in their employment two clerks, one called Perkins and another called Smith. Perkins had an account at one country branch of Lloyds Bank and Smith's wife had an account at another country branch of the same bank.

During a period of five or six years Perkins and Smith stole a number of these crossed bearer cheques and handed them in at one or other of Lloyds Bank London branches, making out pay-in slips which represented that the cheques were paid in by the payees named in the cheques, and directed payment to be made to the credit in some cases of Perkins' account at one country branch and in the other cases to the credit of Smith's wife's account at another country branch. In each case these pay-in slips were sent on by the town branches to the country branches but did not disclose the names of the drawers of the cheques which were sent direct through the clearing.

The brokers sued Lloyds Bank as the collecting bankers for conversion of all the stolen cheques.

The bank pleaded sec. 82 and alleged that they had, in good faith and without negligence, received payment of the cheques for their customers, Perkins and Mrs Smith. The House of Lords, however, found the bank liable.

The Court criticised the bank's practice in dealing with cheques paid in at one branch for the credit of an account kept at another branch, and took the view that the practice was defective in that the branch taking in the cheques did not inform the branch receiving the credit of the names of the drawers of the cheques. Had the branch receiving the credit been made aware of the names of the drawers of the cheques they would or should have been put on their guard and made enquiry as to how such cheques came to be paid in to the credit of the particular account in question.

The Court also criticised the nature and extent of the enquiries which had been made by the country branches when Perkins and Mrs Smith opened their accounts.

Cases like these make depressing reading from the banker's point of view, and as a pleasant change we may turn to two cases with happier endings.

In *Lloyds Bank* v. *Hornby* (1934, Financial Times) the facts were that one Kirkley, whose wife had an account with the bank, presented to them a crossed cheque marked " Account Payee," drawn on Barclays Bank by Hornby and made payable to " F. Kirkley (Fresh Products Ltd.) or order," which he desired should be lodged to the credit of his wife's account. Lloyds Bank declined to do this and Kirkley thereupon obtained in exchange a fresh cheque from Hornby made payable to himself without any reference to

E

Fresh Products Ltd. appearing on it. Lloyds Bank then opened an account in their books in name of Kirkley himself, credited this new cheque to it and allowed Kirkley to draw against it to the extent of £100.

Hornby, after having exchanged the cheques and having become aware of Kirkley's attempt to cash the first cheque, which apparently was a breach of an understanding between the two of them, stopped payment of the second cheque, and Lloyds Bank, as holders for value, sued him for the amount. The defence set up was that the bank were negligent in allowing Kirkley to open an account without making some enquiries about him ; that Kirkley was not a customer and that it was not in order to open an account for the purpose of dealing with a cheque marked " Account Payee."

Mr Justice Branson decided in favour of the bank on the ground that they were not seeking to rely on the protection of the Act, but were suing as holders for value.

" It seems to me [he said] that the bank having kept an account for a married woman who was a respectable and responsible person, it cannot be said that they have been guilty of negligence in opening an account for her husband without making enquiries as to his financial responsibility. To lay down any such rule would be to make it impossible for half the people in the country to open banking accounts."

An unsuccessful attempt was made in Scotland to enlarge and extend the responsibilities of a bank in the case of *Macarthur's Trustees* v. *The Royal Bank* (1933, S.N. 58). There Mr J. J. Paterson, who was the Agent at one of the bank's branches, carried on a house factor's business under the name of J. & W. Paterson. He had an account in this name in the books of the branch where he was Agent, and this being his only account, was used for all his receipts and payments.

Paterson, in connection with his house factor's business, required an overdraft from the bank, who gave him the necessary permission to over-draw. The balance fluctuated, of course, from time to time, but amounted to a considerable sum at the end when the crash came. It then appeared that there had been embezzlement of his client's money and a large sum was outstanding due to various proprietors of property for whom Paterson acted as factor. Rents of these properties had been collected and lodged to the credit of Paterson's overdrawn account, the debit balance on which had been reduced to that extent.

One of these proprietors—Macarthur's Trustees —sued the bank for the amount of the rents collected by Paterson from their property, so far as not previously accounted for, which rents were alleged to have been paid in to the credit of Paterson's overdrawn account. Some of these rents were represented by cheques in favour of Paterson or his firm and some represented by cash. The general ground of the bank's alleged liability was that the knowledge of an Agent being in law equivalent to the knowledge of the principal, the bank must be held to have taken money which they knew to belong to Macarthur's Trustees and applied it in reducing the debt due to themselves by Paterson—in other words, con-verted it and diverted it to their own use. To put it another way—Paterson being the bank, the bank was Paterson and carried on a house factor's business using clients' money as their own.

The Lord Ordinary (Wark) decided that Paterson's knowledge was not to be imputed to the bank in the circumstances and that the bank were not responsible to Macarthur's Trustees —the ground in law being that, where an Agent has information which it is his duty to hand on to his principal and where the Agent has a personal interest not to disclose that information to his principal and does not in fact do so, such knowledge is not to be imputed to the principal by reason of the fact that the Agent knew something which it was not his interest to disclose and which he did not disclose.

One would naturally expect that the bank would have surmised that most of the money being credited to Paterson's account represented rents collected for his other principals as property owners, but the same applies to any other house factor's business although the bank through their Agent in these cases could not identify any particular cheque or sum as relating to any particular property owner. This leads one further and to ask what then is the position of, say, Law Agents whose banking transactions also are mostly represented by clients' money, but which money in many cases is actually earmarked as the property of a specifically named client. Deposit receipts taken out in name of a solicitor and expressed to be in trust for a named client are daily cashed by the solicitor and the proceeds credited to his own current account. Is it negligence on the part of the bank to allow that to be done, and does it make any difference whether the solicitor's account is overdrawn or is at credit at the time ? In view of the general practice contrasted with the various decisions to which I have referred the position is far from clear or satisfactory so far as Scotland is concerned.

Speaking of this matter it is interesting to note

in passing that the Solicitors Act of 1933, relating only to England, provides for the keeping by a solicitor there of a separate bank account for his clients' moneys—usually styled "client account"—and contains a valuable provision in the interest of banks. I think I cannot do better than quote to you part of sec. 8 of that Act, which is as follows :—

" Subject to the provisions of this section, no bank shall, in connection with any transaction on any account of any solicitor kept with it or with any other bank (other than an account kept by a solicitor as trustee for a specified beneficiary), incur any liability or be under any obligation to make any enquiry or be deemed to have any knowledge of any right of any person to any money paid or credited to any such account which it would not incur or be under or be deemed to have in the case of an account kept by a person entitled absolutely to all the money paid or credited to it."

This enactment may be regarded as well conceived and a step in the right direction—that is, of lessening the unreasonable extent of legal responsibility recently shown to attach to bankers, although acting quite innocently and *bona fide*—and has already been the subject of litigation.

The case in question is *Plunkett* v. *Barclays Bank Ltd.* (1936, 2 K.B. 107), which concerned an English solicitor who had opened a "client account" in compliance with the Act and drew a cheque on it to pay rent and costs due by a client to a third party. Before the cheque was presented, however, a garnishee order nisi—the equivalent of an arrestment in Scotland—was served on the bank in order to arrest the sums at the credit of the solicitor's account with them for a private debt of his own. The cheque was consequently returned unpaid and marked " Refer to drawer," and the solicitor claimed damages for alleged libel. It was held that the money at credit of the " client account " was a debt owing by the bank to the solicitor and that the garnishee order attached that debt in the hands of the bank who were, therefore, justified in returning the cheque unpaid and, in the circumstances, the words " Refer to drawer " were not libellous.

A corresponding Act entitled the Solicitors (Scotland) Act, 1933, was also passed for Scotland at the same time, but curiously enough it contains no provision whatever with reference to a solicitor's bank account or the responsibilities of the banker in connection therewith, so that the banker in Scotland is at a disadvantage in this respect as compared with his brother in England. There is, however, at present before Parliament another Bill applicable to Scotland which, as it stands, contains provisions in similar terms to the English Act of 1933 as regards Solicitors' Bank Accounts, and accordingly this disadvantage of Scots bankers will probably be rectified shortly.

I think that banks have a good ground of complaint against the present position as disclosed by cases like those of Slingsby and Savory, because they are apparently expected to investigate their own customers' private and business relationship and connections and antecedents, not for the benefit of that customer or of any of their other customers but for the benefit of the customers of another bank with whom they should have no concern. In the cases mentioned the possibility of negligence on the part of the drawers of the cheques themselves appears to be of minor import- ance, notwithstanding that the drawers were held to be negligent in the cases of Macmillan & Arthur and Gow Bros. & Gemmell. In the Slingsby cases, apart from the drawers' carelessness in filling up, or rather omitting to fill up, the space for the payees' name, one would have been inclined to suppose that, if there were any question of banker's negligence, it was on the part of the Westminster Bank, the collecting bankers, who, however, escaped liability, and not on the part of the District Bank, the paying bankers, who were held liable.

It is not an easy matter to obtain legislation to ameliorate the banker's position, as has already been experienced, and the alternative for the time being would apparently be to make an endeavour to contract out of some at least of the daily risks. A good deal of contracting out is already done by banks to avoid coming under the operation of the law in several respects. For example, the guarantee form is practically nothing else than a contracting out on the part of the bank of numerous rules of law which would otherwise operate to their disadvantage. Since *Crerar* v. *The Bank of Scotland* (1921, S.C. 736) decided that a banker was in the general case bound to return to his customer the identical shares which had been pledged, the banks contract out of that obligation by a suitable clause in the letter of pledge. Since *Coats* v. *The Union Bank* (1929, S.C. (H.L.) 114) decided that several signatories of a cheque were not necessarily jointly and severally liable thereon, the banks make sure that they are now so liable by taking a letter from them on the opening of the credit under which they admit joint and several liability.

Under the Slingsby and Savory cases, we are now faced with extended duties and responsibilities not hitherto contemplated, which are incompatible with the reasonable and prudent activities of a bank to-day and militate against the smooth working of the various facilities offered to the customers. It, therefore, seems desirable that consideration should be given to some method of contracting out of the more serious banking risks existing to-day which cannot reasonably be avoided, and particularly the possibility of confining within limits the apparently boundless expanse of negligent conduct on the part of a banker in acts of honest commission as well as omission.

LECTURE III.

In the first lecture we considered the definition
and requisites of a valid cheque, and it is unnecessary to do more now than to remind you that
the essential difference between a cheque and a
bill of exchange is that a cheque must be drawn
on a banker and be payable on demand, while a
bill may or may not be drawn on a banker and
may or may not be payable on demand.

Practically all the provisions of the 1882 Act
relate to bills as well as cheques, and consequently
most of the observations made in the previous
lectures with regard to cheques are equally applicable to bills, so that now we need only consider
some of the outstanding specialties relating to
bills alone. Time does not permit of these being
dealt with at any great length, but, in any case,
bills are not now of the importance which they
used to be, and as the language of the Act is clear
and simple there will usually be little difficulty
in your being able to decide most of the ordinary
points for yourselves.

A bill requires a different stamp duty from
that on a cheque, and this, with one exception,
is chargeable on an *ad valorem* basis of 1s. per
cent with a scale appropriate to fractions where
the sum is £75 or under. This duty must be
represented by a specially appropriated stamp

known as a bill or note stamp, and not by a
revenue or postage stamp.

This observation, however, does not apply to
a bill drawn payable on demand, or at sight or
on presentation or within three days after date
or sight, or in which no time for payment is
expressed. Such a bill is liable to a fixed duty
of 2d., and this must be represented by an ordinary
revenue stamp—like that found on a cheque—
or a postage stamp and not by a bill stamp. A
2d. bill stamp is only applicable to a bill for £5
or under drawn at a currency and not to a bill
payable on demand. On the other hand, a promissory note payable on demand must be written
on the usual appropriated *ad valorem* bill stamp.

The stamp duty on a foreign bill is represented
by an adhesive foreign bill or note stamp which
requires to be affixed and cancelled before the
bill is presented or negotiated in this country.
Foreign bills payable on demand must not have
an adhesive foreign bill or note stamp for 2d.
affixed thereon, but should have the ordinary
postage or revenue stamp instead. Foreign demand
bills and inland demand bills are exactly in the
same category as regards the stamp. Bills at a
currency, however, must bear the appropriated bill
or note stamp, inland or foreign, as the case may be.

Inland demand bills, however, are not infrequently written on a 2d. bill stamp in error.
Where in such a case as that the correct amount
of duty has been paid but a stamp of the wrong
denomination has been used, the proper stamp
will be impressed by the Inland Revenue on
payment of the duty, and a penalty of 40s. if the
bill has not yet become payable according to its
tenor, but, if it has so become payable, the penalty
is £10.

The definition of a bill of exchange in the Stamp Acts is much wider than that contained in the 1882 Act, and includes many classes of document which no banker would think of calling a bill of exchange. It is not necessary, however, for us to consider this differentiation in the present connection, but I should draw your attention to the fact that the definition of what is an inland bill and what is a foreign bill also differs in the Stamp Acts and in the 1882 Act.

Under the 1882 Act an inland bill is one which is, or on the face of it purports to be (*a*) both drawn and payable within the British Islands or (*b*) drawn within the British Islands upon some person resident therein. Any other bill is a foreign bill in terms of that Act. The British Islands in this connection include the Isle of Man and the Channel Islands, and, of course, Ireland.

For stamp duty purposes, however, a bill which purports to be drawn or made out of the United Kingdom is a foreign bill. Any other bill is an inland bill as regards the stamp. In this connection the Isle of Man and the Channel Islands are not part of the United Kingdom, as they have their own revenue laws. So also has the Irish Free State, subject to certain reciprocal provisions as regards certain forms of taxation.

In this way you may have a bill which is an inland bill for the purposes of the 1882 Act and at the same time is a foreign bill for stamp duty purposes.

A bill may be expressed to be payable with interest—the amount of the interest being left to be calculated at maturity—but this does not affect the amount of the stamp duty which is chargeable only on the principal sum. If, however, the amount of the interest is stated in the bill, then the stamp duty should be calculated on the total amount of the principal sum plus the amount of the interest so stated. There does not appear to be any good reason for this distinction, but it is probably based on the fact that on non-payment at maturity interest will be charged thereafter not only on the principal sum but also on the stated amount of interest, while in the case of a bill with interest—the amount not being stated—the interest due after the date of maturity would be calculated on the simple basis on the principal sum in the bill.

The occasions upon which you are called upon to handle bills of exchange are usually—(1) when a customer hands to you for collection on his behalf a bill which he has drawn and has had accepted or which has been endorsed to him, and (2) when a customer of yours has accepted a bill drawn on him and which he has domiciled with you.

To take the latter case first, there is a general duty on a banker to honour the acceptances of his customer which have been made payable at the bank, provided, of course, that the banker has sufficient funds in hand to enable him to do so. Payment must be made to the person who can give a valid discharge for the money, which means that the onus of seeing that everything is in order is thrown upon the banker, and if he makes a mistake, even in *bona fide* and without negligence, and pays to the wrong person, say on a forged indorsement, he is liable for the loss and cannot debit the amount to his customer's account.

That is a serious responsibility and one which you should endeavour to avoid wherever possible, either by getting your customers to domicile their acceptances elsewhere—say at their own addresses—and retire them if need be by a guaranteed cheque or by your making a special arrangement with them under which they agree to give you the same protection as you would have had under sec. 60, which you will remember relates only to demand bills drawn on a banker.

If, however, in any case where you do not have express instructions from your customer as to the payment of his acceptances, and cannot get into touch with him at the time, you will, of course, make sure of the position, as far as you can, by seeing that, *ex facie*, the bill is all in order and that there is nothing to which objection may be taken later on the part of your customer.

In the drawing and acceptance of bills many irregularities take place, and these sometimes give rise to difficulties which have to be faced on presentment to you for payment. For example, there may be unauthenticated alterations or additions. A not uncommon case is where the acceptor has simply put his signature immediately below that of the drawer without the word " accepted," and across the bill somewhere is written or typewritten the words " payable at the X Bank, Glasgow." There is nothing to show that that addition as to the place of payment was placed on the bill before acceptance and with the knowledge of the acceptor, but, generally speaking, and in the absence of any special circumstances, you will be safe in assuming that the bill is in order and properly domiciled with you.

Another case which occasionally happens is that of the impossible date. One bill brought to my notice was drawn at one month after date and actually bore the date 31st November 1933. One can only make a guess at the due date of payment in a case of that kind, but, where a drawer makes out his document in such a careless way, or an indorsee takes such a carelessly drawn bill, he should not be disappointed if he meets with trouble when presentment to the bank is made for payment. There can be no responsibility on the banker if he refuses to pay on such a document.

Then there are also the difficulties which arise in connection with signatures. In particular, you should be careful of signatures adhibited on behalf of a limited company. These may take almost any form, and what you have to make sure of is that the particular form of execution used in any given case is in accordance with the company's Articles and the instructions of the directors following thereon. This is particularly so when you are to rely upon the validity of the bill from this point of view, as in discounting, &c.

When dealing with the presentment to you for payment of a bill which has properly been domiciled with you, it will be kept in mind that it operates as an intimated assignation of any funds in your hands belonging to your customer— the acceptor of the bill. Sec. 53 refers only to funds in the hands of the drawee and, of course, you are not the drawee of the bill in a case of that kind. It is your customer who is the drawee. The Court have held, however, in the case of *The British Linen Bank* v. *Rainey's Trustee* (1885, 12 R. 825), that the drawee's acceptance amounts to an irrevocable mandate to you to make payment on the date due, and that this is in effect the same as a cheque drawn on you by the acceptor in favour of the billholder and presented for payment. Consequently, it is necessary for you

to make a transfer to a separate account as you
do in the case of a cheque when you have insufficient funds. If, for any good reason, you refuse
payment of a customer's acceptance which has
been domiciled with you, you will, of course, give
the correct answer according to the circumstances,
and advise your customer of what you have done.

The answer to be given by you to the billholder
when for any reason you do not make payment
will, of course, be carefully framed according to
the circumstances and so as not to involve yourselves in awkward questions with your customer
on account of having prejudiced his position and
so on. But whatever the answer may be, it all
resolves in this, that the bill is unpaid and is
noted accordingly, and the notary in making
out his formal protest does so on the simple ground
that payment was refused, or that he could find
no one authorised to pay or to refuse payment.

In *Prince de Bearn* v. *La Compagnie D'Assur-
ances La Federale de Zurich* (42 Com. Cases 189),
bills had been accepted by a firm the constitution
of which was subsequently altered by the retiral
of one of the partners and the admission of a
new partner in his place. The firm as thus altered
became bankrupt later on, and it was held that,
although the holders had ranked for a small
dividend in the bankruptcy, they were not precluded from suing the retired partner for the
balance. The reason for this was that there had
been no arrangement between the retiring partner,
the firm, and the holders to release the retiring
partner from liability and to treat the new firm
as solely liable for the bills.

Turning now to the other case where you are
instructed by a customer to collect a bill for him,
you do not require to be so particular as to whether

the bill is all in order and without any irregularity, as you are only acting as his agent in the matter and are responsible only for carrying out your instructions. On the other hand, if, owing to the state of your customer's account, you require to rely upon the due collection of the money, you will naturally see that the bill is all in order.

Where you have undertaken to collect a bill for a customer it is your duty to carry out the transaction properly, and see that you do nothing to prejudice your customer's position. For example, a customer is entitled to expect that you will, without express instructions, have the bill noted if it is not honoured so as to lay the foundation for summary diligence at a later date.

On the other hand, when you receive for collection a bill having a slip attached to it bearing the words "no expenses," or some equivalent expression, you do not require to note such a bill for non-payment if it has been sent to you by some other bank or office in Scotland, because they may be assumed to mean what they say and know of the legal result. It is quite different, however, when you receive for collection a bill with such a slip attached from a bank in England. In that country noting and protest are of little or no value and summary diligence is unknown. Consequently the instruction " no expenses " may, in these cases coming from England, be assumed to be given in ignorance of the valuable right of summary diligence if noting takes place on dishonour. You should, therefore, if time permits, inform your correspondent of his rights and ask for a reconsideration of such instructions.

In connection with the date on which a bill becomes due, you must take into account the provision in sec. 14 for the three days of grace which are allowed, except in the case of demand or sight bills or bills which expressly stipulate otherwise.

Thus a bill dated 1st January payable three months after date does not mature until 4th April. If the last day of grace falls on Sunday, Christmas Day, Good Friday, or a day appointed by Royal Proclamation as a public fast or thanksgiving day, the bill is due and payable on the preceding business day. But when the last day of grace is a bank holiday (other than Christmas Day or Good Friday) under the Bank Holidays Act, 1871, and Acts amending it, or when the last day of grace is a Sunday and the second day of grace is a bank holiday, then the bill is due and payable on the succeeding business day.

You will notice that sec. 45 contains the rules with regard to presentment for payment. These rules provide that a bill must be duly presented for payment, and if not so presented the drawer and indorsers—not the acceptor—are discharged. Presentment must, in addition to being made at the proper place, be also made on the proper date, which in the case of a bill not payable on demand is the day on which it falls due.

So far as Scotland is concerned there is a difference which you should note. In the case of *M'Neill & Son* v. *Innes, Chambers & Co.* (1917, S.C. 540) it has been held by the Court of Session that as presentment for payment is not required to fix an acceptor with liability it is not necessary that a bill should be presented on the due date as laid down by sec. 45. In a case of that kind in Scotland it is sufficient if presentment is made at any time within six months after the date when the bill falls due. If so presented and noted, summary diligence will be competent against the acceptor but not against any indorsers, notwithstanding the apparent failure to comply with sec. 45.

A bill which is dishonoured by non-acceptance or non-payment may be noted in terms of sec. 51, and, if it is intended to enforce payment by summary diligence, it must be noted. This noting, which is merely a part of the procedure of protesting, is a record made by a notary at the time and forms the foundation for the formal protest which is made out afterwards, if required. Under the 1917 Act the bill may be noted on the day of dishonour and must be noted not later than the next succeeding business day. The day of dishonour in Scotland is the date of the presentment whether on the due date in terms of sec. 45 or at any time within six months thereafter in terms of the decision in *M'Neill & Son* v. *Innes, Chambers & Co.*

The presentment of the bill must, of course, be made at the place where it is payable according to its tenor. If no particular place of payment is specified, then presentment must be made at the place of business or residence of the acceptor, and, if there are two or more acceptors, presentment must be made to each of them.

If there is no notary at the place where the bill is dishonoured, any householder or substantial resident may, in the presence of two witnesses, give a certificate signed by them attesting the dishonour of the bill, and such a certificate takes the place of a formal protest. You should always endeavour, however, so to arrange to obtain the usual notarial protest, as an opinion has been expressed that a householder's certificate does not form a good foundation for summary diligence against the debtor. I should mention, however, that another opinion has been expressed to the opposite effect, but, so far, there is no decision on the point.

That is another aspect of bills which affects Scotland only, just like the presentment of a bill to the drawee having the effect of an intimated assignation. Had these rules been applicable also in England, no doubt we should have had plenty of decisions.

If it is intended to enforce payment by summary diligence, the notary will be asked to write out the usual formal protest against the acceptor and, where required, also against the drawer and indorsers, all jointly and severally. This protest is then registered either in the Sheriff Court Books or the Books of Council and Session, from which, within a few hours, an official extract is issued which has all the attributes of a decree of the Court. Upon this extract the debtor can be charged to make payment within six days, and his assets so far as in his own possession poinded, and those held for him by other persons arrested, and bankruptcy proceedings commenced with the minimum of delay.

Before summary diligence can be authorised, however, it is essential that the bill be complete, regular and proper in all respects, and this is one of the reasons why you should be particular as to the terms of a bill upon which you are relying or which you have discounted. A bill authenticated by the party's initials or mark, or showing an unauthenticated alteration or bearing no date or an impossible date, will not be accepted for this purpose. In the event of non-payment of any bill containing an irregularity of this kind, all that can be done is to raise an ordinary action in Court for payment of the amount, and in such a case, what with dilatory defences and continuations, it may be months before a decree is obtained.

If a bill is not paid when due it will prescribe and become useless as a document of debt in six years in accordance with an old Act of George III. This period of six years runs, in the case of a bill payable on demand, from the date of the bill, and in the case of a bill at a currency from the last day of grace. If, however, the holder of such a bill happens to be in minority during the running of the period, the years of his minority subsequent to his acquisition of the bill are not taken into account, and the six years in that case are accordingly calculated from the date of the holder attaining majority.

The running of this prescriptive period of six years may also be interrupted or stopped by an action being raised or diligence being done on the bill, or by registering the formal protest. Claiming on the bill in a legal process such as a multiple-poinding or sequestration (but not under a trust deed for creditors) is sufficient to interrupt the period. When any such interruption takes place a new period of six years begins to run, but where a formal protest has been registered the period of prescription is twenty years.

If the whole period of the sexennial prescription has been allowed to run, the debt is not thereby extinguished. The only effect is that the bill itself has become useless as a document of debt, and it is necessary for the creditor to prove his debt in some other way. This can only be done by the debtor's writ or oath to the effect that the money is still resting owing. The debtor's writ may be any letter or other writing by him dated subsequent to the expiry of the six years admitting

84

the debt either directly or by clear implication. If the writing is dated during the running of the six years it is useless for this purpose. If the creditor has no suitable writing from his debtor, he may refer the matter to the debtor's oath— that is, he raises an ordinary action for payment of the money, and the debtor is then put in the witness-box and examined on oath as to the borrowing of the money and its repayment or non-repayment. If the creditor is to succeed, he must get the debtor to admit not only that the money was borrowed but also that it is still resting owing. The debtor, however, may admit having borrowed the money, but he may also assert that it was repaid, or he may merely say that he cannot remember, in which case the creditor loses the action.

Before leaving the subject of bills, I should perhaps say a few words regarding the ordinary bank draft. These did not originally come within the 1882 Act, as they are not addressed by one person to another but are drawn by one branch or office upon another branch or office of the same bank. This, however, has been altered by the 1932 Act, and the position now is that the crossed cheque sections of the 1882 Act apply to these drafts as if they were cheques. To come within the 1932 extension, however, they must be payable on demand. Accordingly, these drafts, if on demand, may now competently be crossed, and secs. 80 and 82 of the 1882 Act provide protection for the paying and collecting offices.

You will, of course, observe that it is only the crossed cheque sections which have been made to apply to these demand drafts. The other sections of the Act do not apply, because these drafts have not been brought within the definition of a bill of exchange as given in sec. 3. There may have been good reasons for not including such a draft within that definition, but the result of the omission is somewhat curious. For example, it is only under sec. 29 that one can be a holder in due course with a better title than his author, yet that section does not apply to a bank draft. Consequently, no one can become a holder in due course of such a draft. Then again, can payment of such a draft be countermanded? Sec. 75, even if it did apply, only relates to the stoppage of cheques drawn on a banker by his customer. Further, the protection afforded to the banker under sec. 60, where there is no crossing, does not apply, although sec. 19 of the 1853 Act probably does apply, so that the bank appears to be protected as against a forged indorsement even although the draft has not been crossed.

Bank drafts, even when drawn by one branch on another, are not, however, always payable on demand. Not infrequently these are issued payable, say, ten days after date or ten days after sight. Sight drafts, which usually come from abroad, of course, require acceptance to fix the date of maturity. Bankers do not usually accept after-date drafts, but pay them on presentation when due. In fact, some bankers' drafts have the words " without acceptance " printed in the body. Such drafts are in a still more anomalous position than demand drafts. They do not come within the 1882 Act as they are not drawn by one person on another. They do not come under the 1932 Act because they are not payable on demand, and they do not come under the 1853 Act for the same reason. The result is that they cannot competently be crossed, and the bank have absolutely no protection against a forged indorsement. The practice, I believe, however, is for banks to issue such drafts to their customers when required, without taking any letter relieving them of responsibility.

On no account should you issue a bank draft payable to bearer on demand, because such a document would require to be treated as a bank note and included in the returns required by the various statutes for stamp duty and other purposes. Bank drafts, therefore, should always be made payable to or to the order of a specified person and not to bearer.

We now come to the last subject of these lectures —viz., deposit receipts. Money paid to a banker on deposit is a loan to the banker repayable on demand and the deposit receipt is the acknowledgment by the banker of the receipt of the money. The deposit receipt is not a negotiable instrument and is not transferable by indorsement, but the money itself is a debt assignable in the same way as any other debt is assignable.

A deposit receipt, like various other receipts given by bankers, is exempt from stamp duty under the Stamp Act of 1891. The depositor's indorsement of such a document, however, is a receipt within the meaning of that Act and is, therefore, liable to the 2d. receipt duty. That is why the impressed stamp is on the back and not on the face of the document.

The terms in which the deposit receipt is expressed form the basis of the contract between the bank and the depositor, and it is the banker's duty strictly to fulfil the terms of that contract. But I wish to emphasise that, while this is the case as between the bank and the depositor, the terms of the deposit receipt are not to be taken as determining the actual legal ownership of the money so deposited. For example, a deposit receipt may be taken out in name of A. and B., payable to either or the survivor. While both are alive either may indorse the deposit receipt and uplift the money, and on the death of one the other may still indorse the receipt and uplift the money. On the death of both it is the executor of the survivor who alone has the title to uplift the money. But, although the survivor may insist upon receiving the money, it is not necessarily his, and the executor of the deceased depositor may recover from him the portion which belonged to the deceased or even the whole if the money were all his.

That is a point on which a great many people are under a misapprehension. They appear to think that the survivorship expressed in the deposit receipt carries with it the ownership of the money. It does not. The money continues to belong to the original owner, and he or his executor is entitled to recover possession of it from the party who uplifts it from the bank.

So far as the bank are concerned, they are bound by the terms of their contract and cannot take advantage of any knowledge they may have of the real ownership of the money. For example, it was held in the case of *Anderson* v. *North of Scotland Bank* (1901, 4 F. 49) that, where a deposit receipt had been issued in name of A. and B., not being husband and wife, payable to either or survivor, and A. was overdrawn on his current account, the bank could not withhold payment of the sum on deposit receipt if B. should present the deposit receipt indorsed by him, even although the bank thought they knew that the whole of the money in the deposit receipt belonged to A., their debtor. Therefore, you should never rely upon a deposit in joint names like this as being any good as cover for advances to one of the parties. If you desire to hold such a deposit receipt in security, say, of A.'s debt, the deposit receipt should be indorsed by both and handed back to you with a letter from both A. and B. authorising you to hold the sum in the deposit receipt as security of A.'s debt, and to uplift the money and apply it in repayment or reduction thereof at any time you think fit.

A curious position arises in the case of a deposit receipt in the joint names of a husband and wife and payable to either or survivor where the husband has an overdraft with the bank and becomes bankrupt. Notwithstanding the case of *Anderson* v. *The North Bank*, which I have just mentioned, the wife in a case of this kind is not entitled to uplift the deposit receipt on her own indorsement and the bank are entitled to set off the deposit as against the husband's overdraft.

The reason for this is that under the Married Women's Property Act of 1881 any money belonging to a wife which has been lent to her husband or immixed with his money is deemed to be an asset of the husband's estate in bankruptcy. Consequently, if the wife presented a deposit receipt in joint names of her husband and herself and either or survivor, and demanded payment on her own indorsement, the bank would have a good answer for refusing payment because the 1881 Act says it is not now hers but belongs to the trustee on her husband's estate. The only person, therefore, who could uplift the deposit is the trustee for the husband's creditors, and as against a demand for payment to him the bank would be entitled to set off the husband's overdraft. *The National Bank of Scotland Ltd.* v.

Cowan (1893, 21 R. 4) is the authority in this connection, but you will keep in view that unless the husband is bankrupt, *Anderson* v. *The North Bank* will apply and the wife will be entitled to cash the deposit receipt on her own indorsement notwithstanding her husband's overdraft.

If in a case of such a joint deposit in name of A. and B., whether husband and wife or not, and either or survivor, a creditor of A. lodges an arrestment in the hands of the bank, that arrestment will validly attach the money in the deposit receipt, but only to the extent to which it actually belongs to A. As the bank, however, usually have no authentic official information as to whether the money belongs to A. in whole or in part, they would not be in safety in paying the money over to B. on presentation of the deposit receipt indorsed by him. The case of *Copland* v. *The Union Bank* (1909, S.C. 206) is the authority for that. If B. should persist in his demand for payment, the proper course for the bank to adopt is to raise an action of multiple-poinding and allow the Court to determine to whom the money should be paid.

A similar position arises where the bank receive intimation either from A. or from B. that they are not to pay the money to the other. In such a case the bank can only pay on the signature of both, and if there is any trouble in settling the matter an action of multiplepoinding should be raised by the bank.

Before a depositor can withdraw money lodged on deposit receipt he must, of course, fulfil his part of the contract. The usual form of deposit receipt stipulates that when the money is to be uplifted the receipt must be given up indorsed by the depositor. When the deposit receipt has been lost or mislaid the bank can refuse to make payment, but it is usual in such a case to pay the money after a period on receiving a satisfactory indemnity from the depositor or a third party, or both. This indemnity should state definitely that the deposit receipt has been lost, mislaid or accidentally destroyed, and should bind the granters to free and relieve the bank of and from all claims in respect of their having paid the money without delivery of the deposit receipt and also to deliver up the deposit receipt if and whenever its whereabouts are known.

In the case of a deposit receipt in the joint names of A. and B. without any reference to repayment to either or survivor, payment of the money can only be made on an indorsement by both. If one has died the indorsement must be by his executors and also by the survivor.

Care must always be taken in the case of a deceased person who held a deposit receipt, either by himself alone or jointly with others, that a proper Confirmation is exhibited to you showing the deposit receipt as one of the items of the estate. Unless the deposit receipt is so included the executors have no title to the money and must take out and produce to you an Eik or additional confirmation expressly including the item in question before you can safely make payment.

In one instance the deceased had held a deposit receipt in his own name alone and his executors produced a Confirmation in their favour correctly describing the deposit receipt, but only carrying out into the cash column one half of the amount— the other half being said in the Confirmation to be the property of the deceased's wife. This, however, was of no use to the bank, except to the extent of the one half which had been inserted in the cash column, presumably for death duty purposes, and the executors had to be asked to take out an additional Confirmation to complete their title to the other half when they could uplift the whole of the money and account to the widow for whatever proportion she could show to belong to her.

If the deceased depositor has died domiciled in England the probate or letters of administration in favour of the executors will not contain a note of the separate items of the estate, and you have no duty to enquire whether the deposit has been disclosed to the Inland Revenue or not. In such a case, however, you must see that the probate or letters of administration have been duly re-sealed in the Commissary Court in Edinburgh. Unless so re-sealed in this country the document is of no use to you.

The indorsement of a deposit receipt in name of a deceased holder should be by at least a majority of his executors unless the Confirmation expressly provides otherwise. In the case of executors acting under an English probate all must sign, as there is no rule outside Scotland permitting a majority of trustees or executors to act by themselves.

The case may arise of a person dying holding a deposit receipt in name of, say, A. in trust for B., and, in that event, the Confirmation in favour of A.'s executors should show the deposit receipt under the heading of " Funds held in trust." The sole title to uplift such a deposit is vested in the executors of A. B., the beneficiary, for whom the deposit is held, is not in a position to give the bank a discharge for the money.

Where such a trust deposit receipt was held

by a person domiciled, say, in England, the probate
in favour of his executors, provided it be re-sealed
in this country, is sufficient for your purpose
although it makes no reference to the money so
held in trust. The executors of such a deceased
trustee in England become automatically the new
trustees of the deposit, but that is not so in Scotland
where they have no rights in the matter unless conferred by their confirmation as above mentioned.

Where a deceased depositor's whole estate does
not exceed £100, in which case no death duties
are payable, it is usual to pay any sums standing
to the deceased's credit either on current account
or deposit receipt to his next-of-kin or legal
representatives on their granting a discharge
therefor and undertaking to expede Confirmation
at any time if called upon, but you are under
no obligation to follow this course. If you do,
you may run the risk of being asked to pay again
to some other person producing the proper Confirmation. A creditor of the deceased depositor
might take out Confirmation in his own name
and so also might the person who bore the funeral
expenses. So, unless you are perfectly certain,
you should ask that Confirmation be produced to
you in the usual way in every case.

A deposit receipt is not in itself a negotiable
document capable of being transmitted by indorsement so as to confer on the indorsee, by that
act alone, the right of property in the money
represented by the deposit receipt. Consequently,
possession of an indorsed deposit receipt does not
of itself confer on the possessor any right of
property in the money. It merely implies a mandate to uplift the money on behalf of the depositor,
and the death of the depositor cancels that mandate,
so that you cannot cash a deposit receipt in name

of a person now deceased even although it has been indorsed by him. In the case of *Barstow* v. *Inglis & Hay* (1857, 20 M. 230) it was indicated, however, that it might be sufficiently proved that the possessor of such an indorsed deposit receipt had given an onerous consideration for it, in which case the mandate in his favour to uplift would not fall by the death of the depositor. But you should refer any case of this kind to Head Office or to the law agents for advice and not act on your own initiative.

For the reason that the property in a deposit receipt is not transferred by a simple indorsement, you should never accept as security for an advance an indorsed deposit receipt of another bank although you may safely do this with one of your own. Besides, that other bank may have or may later on acquire a lien over the money in the deposit receipt which would form a claim ranking prior to yours. The indorsement of that other bank's deposit receipt is only a mandate which may fall or be cut down for some reason and you may thus lose your supposed security. What should be done is to cash that deposit receipt and issue one of your own in its place and hold that as your security.

If, however, it should be impracticable to do anything else but continue the deposit with the other bank, then you should obtain a proper assignation thereof which should be duly stamped and intimated to the other bank and the usual enquiry made as to whether they have any lien or counterclaim against that money.

In the case of the *Bank of Ireland* v. *Martin* (1937, I.R. 189) the defendant Martin, who had granted a guarantee for £1800 on account of another customer of the bank under which £1390 was due, lodged a sum of £500 on deposit receipt with the bank in his own name on the usual terms. The bank's debtor having failed to make payment of the debit balance on his current account, the bank applied the £500 on deposit receipt towards the debit balance on the guaranteed account, and the Court held that they were not entitled to do so without the consent of the defendant. The Court recognised, however, the right of the bank to set off or to refuse payment of the sum on deposit receipt until the depositor had paid the sums due by him under his guarantee. This decision is, of course, consistent with the general rule that a banker is not entitled at his own hand to move effects or liabilities from one account to another of the same customer although he is entitled to take into account the fact that the credit balance on one account may be diminished or extinguished by the existence of the debit balance on another account unless there is an arrangement to the contrary.

Although the possession of an indorsed deposit receipt generally implies a mandate to the possessor to receive the money, it sometimes is difficult for the banker to determine whether in any given circumstances such a mandate is sufficiently clearly implied to warrant payment being made without enquiry or verification. Where a depositor has over a long period always attended to his own banking transactions and himself uplifted his deposit receipts and one day some person, whom you actually know to be his servant, presents an indorsed deposit receipt and asks payment in cash, you are in somewhat of a difficulty. Strictly speaking, you should not pay cash in such a case, because there is no precedent for your doing so and you have no arrangement with your depositor to that effect. For all you know, the servant demanding the cash may have obtained the indorsed deposit receipt by some improper means or it may be for a specific purpose—say, turning it over and getting a new receipt in the same name to include the interest earned down to date. Consequently, if anything should be wrong, you will be responsible for the loss.

The converse case is that of a depositor who never does any of his banking transactions personally but only by his servant. In such a case, assuming that the course of dealing has been well established, you will be in safety in paying cash in exchange for an indorsed deposit receipt provided that the amount involved or the circumstances surrounding the transaction are not such as to put you on your enquiry.

Where a deposit receipt is presented to you by another banker duly indorsed by your depositor you will be in safety in making payment because you are entitled to assume that that other banker has your customer's authority to uplift the cash. If, however, any question is afterwards raised, the banker presenting the deposit receipt to you for payment must keep you clear as he impliedly warrants not only his authority to act as agent in the matter but also the genuineness of the depositor's indorsement.

Between the extremes of these examples, however, there is a multitude of possible combinations of circumstances regarding which it is difficult to lay down any general rule of practice as regards cashing a deposit receipt for your depositor's messenger. A banker usually requires to study the convenience and wishes of his customer and avoid giving offence, which unfortunately the customer is sometimes only too ready to imagine.

On the other hand, the banker ought not to be expected to run any unnecessary risk in the matter. If there is any risk, it should be taken by the customer, but that is not the real position. Accordingly, in each case where there is any doubt, the banker requires to make up his mind for himself as to whether the risk of anything being wrong or going wrong is one that he can take or one that he should refuse. It is always well, I think, to be on the safe side and refuse payment to a servant or messenger where there is no well established course of dealing. It is much easier, on the one hand, to explain to your customer that it is not suspicion of his servant but anxiety for his own safety that leads you to follow a prudent course than, on the other hand, for you to explain to Head Office how you came to think that you were justified in paying over cash to a messenger which has to be paid over again to the depositor himself.

A deposit receipt not being a negotiable instrument can only be transferred *tantum et tale* as held by the depositor and subject to all liens and counterclaims competent to the bank against him. For example, you may have a counterclaim against the depositor in respect of advances made to him on a current account even although the deposit receipt has not been lodged as security. In such a case, while the depositor may execute a legal assignation of the deposit to some third party, that third party can acquire no higher right than the depositor himself had and your counterclaim is valid against him also, but only to the extent of the advances which you may have made prior to the date when the third party gave you intimation of his assignation.

If such a situation did arise and intimation be

given to you of the granting of such a legal assignation of the deposit, you should at once stop operations on the current account if you wish to retain your right of counterclaim. The reason is that the future debits on the current account will not be claimable against the deposit while all future credits will, in accordance with the rule in Clayton's case, go to reduce the previous advances for which you could counterclaim.

Although not falling within the scope of these lectures I think I should mention that this position arises in connection with any other class of security which you may hold for advances on a current account, and similar steps should be taken for the same reason. For example, if you hold a security for fluctuating advances over your customer's property by way of an *ex facie* absolute disposition or cash credit bond and disposition in security, and receive information that your customer has sold the property or granted a postponed security over it, your future advances will be either unsecured altogether or postponed to the new security. The principle of this rule of law you will find laid down in the case of *The Union Bank* v. *The National Bank*, in 1886.

The bank must exercise due care that they pay the money in a deposit receipt to the proper person as there is no statutory protection available to cover mistakes in this connection. If the indorsement of the deposit receipt, which is the bank's receipt for the money, is forged or if they have paid to the wrong person, they will be liable to pay again. In the case of *Wood* v. *The Clydesdale Bank* (1914, S.C. 397), a depositor who was abroad sent to his brother in this country by registered post an indorsed deposit receipt for £100 along with a letter addressed to the bank asking them to pay the brother £60 of the money. A similar letter was sent to the bank direct. The letter to the bank was duly delivered, but the letter to the brother with the deposit receipt was stolen in transit. A person representing himself to be the depositor's brother presented the indorsed deposit receipt to the bank and received the £60 in cash and a new deposit receipt for the balance in name of the depositor. The depositor thereafter brought an action against the bank for recovery of the money, and judgment was given in his favour as the bank were held to be responsible for seeing that the money was paid to the proper person.

It is an implied term of the contract of deposit that interest will be paid by the bank on the amount, although as a matter of fact the deposit receipt is silent on the subject. The banks from time to time advertise the rate of interest allowed on deposits and no other notice of any change in the rate is given to any depositor. The bank's liability to pay interest and the rate of that interest, however, are sufficiently established by these advertisements and also by use and wont.

The interest is only payable along with the principal sum when the deposit receipt is delivered up indorsed, and, irrespective of the period during which the money has been on deposit, simple interest only is allowed. The general rule of law is that simple interest only is payable in all cases with certain limited exceptions. These exceptions include cases where there is a definite agreement that interest shall be chargeable on a compound basis as in certain commercial dealings ; cases where there is a well and clearly established practice, as in the case of bank overdrafts and cash accounts, and cases where there has been an abuse committed by a party entrusted with money belonging to others.

There is also a statutory exception to the simple interest rule to be found in the Pupils Protection Act, or, as it is sometimes called, the Judicial Factors Act, 1849. In terms of sec. 37 of that Act, every bank in Scotland with which any money has been deposited or lodged by any judicial factor, tutor or curator or under authority of any Court in Scotland or with reference to any suit in any Court in Scotland whether on deposit receipt or current account, must once at least in every year accumulate the interest with the principal sum so that both shall thereafter bear interest together as principal, and any bank failing so to do is liable to account as if such money had been so accumulated.

That is a difficult Act to understand and apply. Notwithstanding its title, its operation has been held not to be limited to pupils or judicial factors. It bears to apply to any money lodged in bank under an order of the Court or with reference to any suit in Court, but that is not very specific and there is little authority on the subject. It is not often that this question arises, and I do not trouble you with the technical considerations to be taken into account in determining whether or not the bank are liable for compound interest in any given case.

In the second lecture I had intended to say something to you with regard to arrestments lodged in the hands of a bank so far as relating to bills, cheques and deposit receipts, but there were so many interesting things to say about cheques I thought it might be as well to leave over dealing with the subject of arrestments till this lecture.

Arrestment is one of various forms of procedure competent to a creditor in Scotland in connection with the enforcement, under a warrant from the Court, of payment of a debt due to him. There are various classes of arrestment appropriate to different sets of circumstances, as, for example—

1. Arrestment to found jurisdiction against a foreigner.
2. Arrestment on the dependence of an action.
3. Arrestment in execution of a decree.
4. Arrestment in security of a debt not yet payable.

The two forms which concern you most are those on the dependence of an action and those in execution of a decree, and as the others are to you more or less academic I shall not deal with them on this occasion.

When a creditor finds it necessary to raise an action against his debtor for payment of money, it does not follow that he can obtain a decree at once because of the possibility of the debtor disputing the claim, appearing in Court, lodging defences—even mere dilatory defences—appealing to a higher Court and so on. Accordingly, the creditor may think it desirable to prevent the debtor, pending a final decree being obtained, from spending or otherwise disposing of his assets or even using all his money in the expenses of the litigation—to the ultimate detriment of the creditor.

To achieve this laudable object the creditor, when taking out the summons, obtains from the Court what is known as a warrant to arrest on the dependence of the action. The summons is then served, and arrestments are lodged in the hands of everybody whom the creditor has reason to believe holds any money or other property belonging to the debtor. These arrestments prevent the arrestees from parting with the money, or property arrested, until the action has been finally disposed of by the Court, when the creditor, if he wins his case, can then proceed under his decree.

Let us assume that an arrestment on the dependence is lodged in your hands to attach funds held by you on account of one of your customers. You will have no difficulty in making out that it is an arrestment on the dependence, as it says so. It also says that it arrests in your hands the sum of, say, £100 more or less belonging to your customer. You will immediately refer to your books to see what various assets of all kinds you hold for that customer. Assume that you have a sum of, say, £200 at the credit of the current account. In accordance with what I said in the previous lecture, you will at once transfer the whole credit balance to a separate account, earmarking it as against this arrestment, and then keep a careful record of your customer's cheques which may thereafter be presented to you, payment of which you will refuse with the answer "refer to drawer." At the same time you will immediately advise your customer of the receipt of the arrestment and tell him what you have done.

Now, although the arrestment bears only to attach the sum of £100 more or less, you must not be misled by that and transfer only that amount to the special account, as the decree to be obtained later on by the creditor may be for more or it may be for less. Consequently, your only safe course is to transfer the whole balance and tell your customer, and leave him to deal with the position.

Of course, if the sums in your hands are con- siderably in excess of the sum mentioned in the arrestment, or if your customer has plenty of money otherwise, you may be prepared to take the risk and transfer only the £100 to the separate account, so as to avoid dishonouring your customer's cheques on account of the relatively small item in dispute.

If, however, you are not inclined to take any risk in the matter, you or your customer can probably arrange for the creditor's solicitor giving you a letter to say that it will be sufficient if you set aside a specified sum against the arrestment, and this will keep you safe notwithstanding the terms of the decree which may be subsequently obtained. Of course, it may be that the Court may recall or restrict the arrestment, in which case a certified copy of the relative interlocutor should be produced to you.

If the creditor should be unsuccessful in his action, the arrestment on the dependence falls, but you should not be satisfied as to that unless you either obtain a letter from the creditor's solicitor to that effect or have produced to you the final decree absolving your customer. When you receive satisfaction in one or other of these forms you will make provision, out of the money previously transferred to the separate account, for the payment in their proper order of the cheques which were presented to you after the arrestment was lodged and retransfer any free balance to your customer's account.

If, on the other hand, the creditor is successful in his action he will, no doubt, proceed further under the decree which he has obtained. He does not require to use arrestments in execution but merely to follow up the arrestment on the dependence with an action of furthcoming.

An arresting creditor who has used an arrestment

on the dependence is not entitled to know whether or not his arrestment has attached any funds in your hands, but, where he has used an arrestment in execution or has obtained a decree, he is entitled to know whether his arrestment has attached anything, and you are bound to give him the desired information. That does not mean, however, that you are to tell him all about your customer's affairs, but only so much as will apparently cover his rights under the arrestment— *i.e.*, his debt, principal and interest, and expenses.

You must not, however, pay anything over to the creditor, even although he has used an arrestment in execution, until he produces a decree in an action of furthcoming entitling him to receive payment from you, unless, of course, your customer consents in writing to your doing so.

If the creditor raises an action of furthcoming you will be called as defenders along with your customer, but you do not require to take any steps in the matter or appear in Court. It is sufficient for you to allow the creditor to obtain a decree in absence against you.

The only occasion when you require to intervene in an action of furthcoming is where the creditor in his summons of furthcoming asks the Court for expenses against you. The summons should bear that he asks expenses against you only in the event of your appearing to defend, but sometimes these qualifying words are omitted, in which case you should obtain from the creditor's solicitor a letter assuring you that he will amend the wording when the case calls in Court. If you cannot obtain such a letter, you will require to be represented in Court to have the matter put right, because you should not be responsible for any such expenses.

The subjects which an arrestment will attach in your hands are sums at the credit of a current account or on deposit receipt or savings account and, in general, all moveable assets which you may hold for your customer, including stock exchange securities, life policies, rights of reversion and so on. An arrestment, however, does not attach bills of exchange or the money contained in them and several other classes of assets. There is, I should mention, room for much argument and litigation on the question of what funds or assets an arrestment will attach in the hands of a bank—such as scrip for stock exchange securities held with unregistered transfers, unintimated assignations and so on, but I do not trouble you with these as they are outside our scope on this occasion.

There is also room for much argument and litigation on the question whether an arrestment of assets belonging to A. is good or bad when, as a matter of fact, such assets stand in the bank's books in the joint names of A. and B., or in name of A in trust for X., or in name of X. in trust for A. There is little authority anywhere on these problems, which will require to be dealt with as and when they arise. Generally speaking, however, the only safe course for a bank to follow, in the first instance, is to regard all assets in their books in which A. is interested in any of these forms as being attached by the arrestment.

It has, however, been held in the Sheriff Court that an arrestment in the hands of a bank of funds belonging to A. attaches money standing in the bank's books in name of A. " in trust," where no specification of the beneficiary is given.

In the two trust examples given above—A. in trust for X. and X. in trust for A.—the solution of the problem as to the effect of an arrestment against A. will probably be found on a determination of the question whether it is a case of a real trust or merely a case of agency subject to an accounting—in other words, who is the legal as distinct from the beneficial owner of the money in question.

I would again draw your attention to the case of *Plunkett* v. *Barclays Bank Ltd.*, where it was held that a garnishee order served on the bank in respect of debts due from the bank to a solicitor attached sums at the credit of a " client account " which had been opened by the solicitor in terms of the English Solicitors Act of 1933.

In another case, *Hirschorn* v. *Evans* in re *Barclays Bank Ltd.* (54 T.L.R. 1069), a joint account had been opened in name of husband and wife to be operated by either, and a garnishee summons was lodged against the husband. It was held that a joint account could not be attached to answer a judgment debt of one of the parties to the account even when the bank was expressly authorised to repay money against the signature of either of them.

An arrestment in the hands of a bank against A. has the effect of attaching funds at the credit of a business or concern in which A. is the sole partner, no matter under what name he is carrying on the business. For example, if John Brown is carrying on business under the name of J. Smith & Co. or the Elite Machinery Co. or anything like that, then an arrestment against John Brown alone without any reference to these trade names will attach all funds in your hands in name of J. Smith & Co. or the Elite Machinery Co., as the case may be. But if John Brown is not the sole partner in the concern the arrestment will not attach the funds standing in your books under these trade names.

On the other hand, an arrestment against J. Smith & Co. or the Elite Machinery Co., of which John Brown is a partner, will attach all funds in your hands standing in name of John Brown as an individual whether he is named in the arrestment or not.

In any case, where there is a real doubt as to whether or not an arrestment has validly attached funds in any of the various sets of circumstances outlined above and parties are not able to agree in such a way as to protect the bank, the proper course is for the bank to take up the position that there are competing claims to the same asset or, as the lawyers say, double distress, and raise an action of multiplepoinding. The funds in dispute are then paid into Court and the bank receive a judicial discharge—the other parties being left to fight out their respective rights and interests in Court.

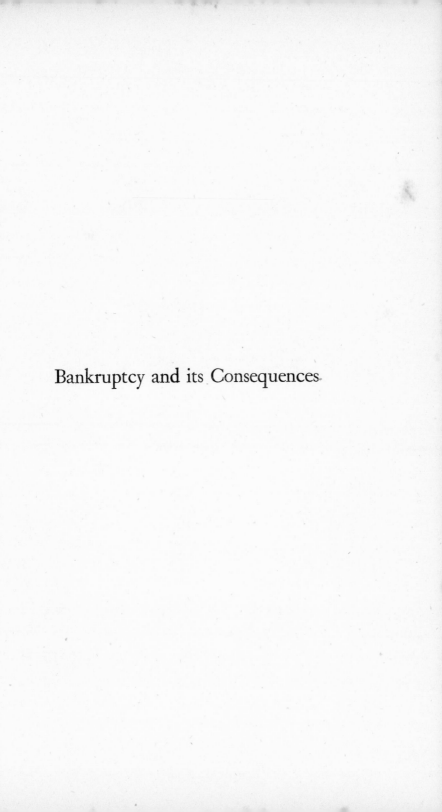

Bankruptcy and its Consequences

LECTURE I.

THIS series of lectures is intended to deal with the position of a banker in connection with the bankruptcy of his customer, not only as regards what follows upon the bankruptcy but also, and very important, as regards what, in the interests of the banker, takes place or ought to have taken place prior to the bankruptcy. As you can appreciate, it is much more important to endeavour in advance, if at all possible, to keep out of trouble of this kind with a customer's affairs than to get out of the trouble once you are in it, and it is from this point of view that I propose to endeavour to treat the subject.

Just in the same way as it was impossible for me in the limited time at our disposal to deal with the whole subject of bills, cheques and deposit receipts, so in the present series it will not be possible to tell you all about bankruptcy and its complications, but I shall endeavour to select and put before you a number of the more common and interesting points generally found to arise in connection with ordinary banking business.

To begin with, I wish to speak to you more particularly with regard to what lawyers call ascription of payments, or, as you probably know it better, specific appropriation, and it is necessary for you to understand the effect of the rules of

law in this connection in order that you may
be enabled, in your previous dealings with your
customer, to keep clear of troublesome questions
which may arise in the event of his becoming
bankrupt at some later date.

It will be sufficient, I think, for our present
purpose, if I content myself by saying that, shortly
stated, according to our law, a debtor who owes
several debts to the same creditor has the first
option, when making a payment to account to
his creditor, to appropriate the payment to any
one of these debts. No creditor is bound to
accept a part payment, but, if he does, he must
accept with it the debtor's appropriation thereof.
The creditor's only alternative is to refuse to
accept the partial payment and demand the whole
debts.

An appropriation by the debtor, however, if
the creditor does not refuse the part payment,
must, in order to be effectual, be specific, and it
must be made by the debtor at the time he makes
the payment. He cannot afterwards attempt to
make such an appropriation.

If no such appropriation is made by the debtor
at the time of payment, then the creditor may
make the appropriation and apply the payment
to such of the debts as he pleases. For example,
if one debt is secured and another is not, or if
one is better secured than the other, the creditor
may appropriate the payment to the unsecured
or least secured debt even although this may in
the end be to the prejudice of the debtor's other
creditors. The same applies where, for example,
one debt is carrying interest and the other is not.
The creditor's right to make an appropriation of
a part payment differs from the debtor's right
in this respect, in that he—the creditor—may

exercise his right of appropriation either at the time he receives the payment or at any later date.

The creditor may carry out and communicate to the debtor such appropriation in several ways, either expressly or by implication, as, for example, by expressly informing the debtor either at the time or later on as to what he has done, or, on the other hand, by implication, by making up and rendering to the debtor accounts giving effect to the appropriation, that is, showing in his statement of accounts that he has credited the payment to one particular debt. Once appropriation has taken place in one or other of these ways, however, the creditor is not entitled afterwards to make any change or transfer the credit from one account to another.

These observations relate, you will notice, to cases where there are several separate debts or items, but other considerations apply where the debts cannot be treated as separate but fall to be dealt with together as one single debt, such as the balance arising on any current account between two parties in the position, for example, of banker and customer. Here a different rule of appropriation applies to the several items on each side of the account and in the absence of any agreement between the parties, the law steps in and makes a special appropriation of its own.

Approximately 125 years ago, there died a gentleman called William Devaynes who was a banker in London carrying on business in partnership with four others under the name of Devaynes, Dawes, Noble & Co. A few months after Devaynes' death the remaining partners in that banking house became bankrupt, and, following upon these two events, considerable litigation ensued with the object principally of ascertaining how far the estates of the late Mr Devaynes or his representatives were responsible to the customers and other creditors of the house in respect of moneys owing to them and which they had lost in consequence of the bankruptcy.

The decision of the Court in these litigations is reported under the name of *Devaynes* v. *Noble* (1 *Merivale's Reports* 529). Quite a number of customers of the house came forward claiming that Devaynes' estate and his representatives, who were then the only solvent parties connected with the business, should be held liable for the loss of the money, &c., which they had had at their credit with the house at the time Devaynes died. These customers were all claiming under different circumstances and on different grounds—some in respect of investments and securities which had been in the custody of the house, some in respect of bills, some in respect of deposits and current account balances and so on. One of those who claimed in respect of a current account balance was a Mr Clayton, whose name has attached itself to his part in the litigation and has thereby become to all intents and purposes immortal. The rule as to specific appropriation laid down in Clayton's case is one that will survive so long as there are such things as current accounts. Other branches of this great litigation are known as Sleech's case, Baring's case, Houlton's case, and so on, but for our present purposes these do not concern us.

At the date of Devaynes' death, Clayton was a customer of the house and had a balance at his credit of £1713. He was, therefore, a creditor of the house to that extent, and Devaynes, being a partner of the house, was responsible therefor, as was also the considerable fortune which he had left. In that position of matters, Clayton, within a few days after Devaynes' death, drew out of his account with the house, which was being carried on as before by the surviving partners, a sum of £1260, which reduced his credit balance considerably, and naturally reduced the liability of Devaynes' estate. After that, Clayton had various operations on the account by way of both paying in and drawing out. The total of the amounts which he drew out exceeded the £1713 which he had had at his credit at the date of Devaynes' death, but, with the new lodgments which he had made after that date, there was still a balance at his credit of about the same amount when the house failed some months later.

In these circumstances Clayton put forward a claim against Devaynes' estate for £1171, being the balance of the original £1713 remaining after crediting the dividends which he had received from the bankrupt partners' estates. The Court, however, held that the whole of the original £1713, for which Devaynes was originally legally liable to Clayton, had, through the subsequent withdrawals from the account, been paid back to Clayton by the surviving partners, and that the sum at his credit at the date of the subsequent bankruptcy was the total of the lodgments he had made to the credit of the account after Devaynes' death, and with which Devaynes or his estate could not possibly have had anything to do. In other words, the balance at the date of the bankruptcy was a new and a different debt incurred to Clayton by the surviving partners and by them alone.

In this case the Court in effect held that, in applying the principle of appropriation to a current account, the just and equitable thing to do was to say that, in the absence of any other appropriation being made by either party, each payment by the debtor must be regarded as wiping out the debit items in the order of their date. In other words, the earliest items on the debit side of a current account are extinguished as and when and to the extent to which payments are made to the credit side of the account.

One of the leading cases in Scotland as to the application of this principle of appropriation in the case of a current account is that of *Christie* v. *Royal Bank* (1841, 2 Rob. 118). In that case Thomas Allan, who was one of the partners of a firm called Allan & Son, joined with his partners in giving to the bank a cash credit bond for certain advances to the firm in which was incorporated a disposition in security by Thomas Allan in favour of the bank of the estate of Lauriston which belonged to himself as an individual.

Shortly afterwards Thomas Allan died, at which time there was a balance of £8800 due by the firm to the bank on the current account, and the bank, without taking any special notice of his death—to them a most important event—carried on the same current account with the surviving partners under the same firm name without making any change. Thereafter the remaining partners of the firm were made bankrupt while still indebted to the bank.

Christie and others, who were creditors of Thomas Allan as an individual, thereupon raised an action against the bank with the view of depriving the bank of the benefit of the security which they held under their cash credit bond and disposition in security, and pleaded, in addition to certain technical objections with which we are not concerned, that the principle laid down in Clayton's case applied, and that, through the operations on the account after the death of Thomas Allan and the payments since then made to the credit of that account, the £8800 which had been outstanding at that date had since been repaid to the bank, and that the balance due to the bank at the date of the firm's bankruptcy was a new debt afterwards incurred by the surviving partners alone and therefore not a debt for which Thomas Allan could possibly be responsible and therefore not secured by the cash credit bond. The Court held that that was so, and that the bank had, in these circumstances, lost their claim against Thomas Allan's estate for the £8800 due to them at the time of his death and also the security which they held therefor over the estate of Lauriston.

In the case of the *Union Bank* v. *National Bank* (1886, 14 R. (H.L.) 1), Mrs M'Arthur had, in security of advances from them, given to the National Bank an *ex facie* absolute disposition of her property in Greenock coupled with the usual back letter. Thereafter she granted to the Union Bank an assignation of her reversionary right and interest in that property in security of advances made and to be made by them. The Union Bank thereupon sent to the National Bank a formal intimation of the fact that Mrs M'Arthur had now granted to them that assignation of her reversionary interest, but to this the National Bank paid no attention. Both banks thereafter made advances to Mrs M'Arthur, and when the crash came, the Union Bank, founding upon the case of *Hopkinson* v. *Rolt* (1861, 9 H.L.C. 514), and other cases, took up the position that the National Bank's security over the property was limited to the amount which they had advanced at the date when they received the intimation of the Union Bank's assignation. The House of Lords decided in favour of the contentions put forward by the Union Bank and held that the National Bank could not recover out of the property any more than the debt which had been due to them at the date when they received intimation of the Union Bank's postponed security.

In this connection reference may be made to the case of *Deeley* v. *Lloyds Bank Ltd.* (1912, A.C. 756). In this case John Glaze granted to the bank a mortgage over his property to secure all sums due and to become due by him to the bank up to a maximum of £2500. Two years afterwards, when the debit balance due to the bank was £3379, Glaze borrowed money from another creditor, Deeley, and gave him a mortgage postponed to that held by the bank, and Deeley, following the usual practice in England, where there is no real registration of title to property, sent formal intimation to the bank of the granting of the second mortgage in his favour, to which, however, the bank paid no attention. Later on Glaze became bankrupt, by which date his debit balance had considerably increased. The bank thereafter sold the security subjects and claimed to retain the whole of the proceeds of sale to account of their debt. Deeley, as second mortgagee, however, raised an action against them and pleaded first of all that the notice which he had given to the bank when he obtained the second mortgage was sufficient to prevent the bank thereafter making further advances to the debtor to the prejudice of Deeley's mortgage and that the bank's claim against the security subjects was limited to the £3379 due to them at the date of the intimation, and founded upon, amongst others, the case of *Union Bank* v. *National Bank*, which I have just mentioned. That was a bad enough position for the bank to be in, but Deeley went still further and pleaded that the principle of appropriation as applied in Clayton's case applied here also, and that in the subsequent operations on the account the payments which had been made to the credit were to be imputed in satisfaction of the £3379 which had been outstanding at the date when his intimation was given to the bank. The House of Lords decided in favour of Mr Deeley.

The rule laid down in Clayton's case as to general appropriation on a current account is not an absolute rule that must be applied to every such account. It is quite possible for the parties to agree either expressly or impliedly that the rule in Clayton's case is not to apply but that some other method of appropriation is to apply instead.

As an example of such an agreement you will find in the guarantee forms of certain of the English banks a clause expressly providing that on the happening of any event which in law would have the effect of drawing a line across the account in a question with the guarantor, the bank are nevertheless entitled to continue the operations on the same account without any right on the part of the guarantor to say that the subsequent lodgments are, in accordance with Clayton's rule, to be applied in reducing the previous debit entries for which he is responsible.

That is an agreement for a special appropriation of subsequent lodgments, as against the subsequent withdrawals, and obviates the necessity for opening a new separate account for these.

Any agreement along these lines can be made between the parties and will receive effect provided it is clear, but, of course, where there is no such agreement, the rule in Clayton's case will apply.

In the case of *Macdonald, Fraser & Co.* v. *Cairns's Executor* (1932, S.C. 699), the pursuers were creditors of the late Mr Cairns at the date of his death. Under an arrangement with them, the widow, who was also executor dative, carried on the deceased's farm for the next four years, all purchases and sales of stock being made through the pursuers who financed the farming operations and rendered termly accounts to the executor showing the debit and credit items. At the date of the action there was still a balance due to the pursuers, but the amounts credited as proceeds of sales exceeded the amount of the original debt. It was held that the rule in Clayton's case did not apply as this would have been contrary to the intention of the parties, which was the gradual extinction of the debt due by the deceased by the application of the profits made from the working of the farm and the realisation of stock, as evidenced by the arrangement between the parties. In other words, the Court held that the intention of the parties was that the original debt due by the deceased was only to be regarded as paid off from time to time by the net profits and not by the gross receipts of the business.

So far, the cases with which we have been dealing were cases where the rule laid down in Clayton's case had been allowed by the banks to come into operation to their detriment, but there are circumstances where it is to the advantage of the bank that the rule in Clayton's case should definitely be allowed to come into operation, and it is frequently of great importance to the banker to know when to open a new account, and when not to do so. I hope to be able to deal with this important point later, and in the meantime would content myself by referring to one recent case where there was a dispute as to whether the rule as to appropriation laid down in Clayton's case applied, or whether another specific appropriation by agreement was applicable instead.

The case is that of *The National Provincial Bank Ltd.* v. *Freedman*, 1934, which is not officially reported, and which, by the way, illustrates the danger of the use of words which are none too clear, or which, on the other hand, are capable of a double meaning, particularly in this question of specific appropriation as against a particular item, or general appropriation in accordance with Clayton's rule.

In this case a limited company—Bach Ltd.— had an overdraft account with the bank. Towards the end—just before the company went into liquidation—the bank's head office, being apparently apprehensive of the increasing debit, instructed their branch manager that the account was not to be allowed to go beyond a fixed limit, which meant that the customers were compelled to work on a hand-to-mouth basis. They required money every week to meet the wages of their employees, and the branch manager accordingly would not, and did not, cash the wages cheques until he was satisfied that there was being contemporaneously paid in, or would be paid in during the course of a few hours, cheques in favour of the customers which would have the effect of reducing the overdraft to such an extent that the wages cheques would not, when put through, increase the overdraft beyond the prescribed limit. So what the company did was to gather up the cheques received by them during each week and then lodge them to the credit of the account at the same time as they cashed the wages cheque—thus complying strictly with the requirements of head office.

On the company going into liquidation the bank claimed a preferential ranking, under sec. 264 of the Companies Act of 1929, for the wages cheques which they had cashed for a number of weeks before, but the liquidator took up the position that the bank had advanced no money to meet these wages, because, he said, the cash they had paid out on the wages cheques was merely the same cash which had been lodged at the same time to the credit of the account to enable these wages cheques to be met—in other words, that the company just handed in their cheques to the bank, who gave them cash in exchange therefor ; and that that was the money which paid for the wages and that no advance was made by the bank for that purpose as provided by the Act.

Mr Justice Clauson, who tried the case, in the course of his opinion, said :—

" There is a suggestion that there were conversations of a somewhat loose character from which it can be inferred that there was an arrangement that the cheques paid in were to be used simply to provide the cash to pay the wages. What seems to me to be most important is the way in which the account was kept. The way the account was kept shows perfectly clearly that that was not the transaction at all. The transaction was that those cheques reduced the overdraft, and that is the meaning of the bank account as it appears. The bank manager, whatever loose language he may have used, was not going to let the overdraft be permanently increased, and accordingly it was necessary for him to take care that the wages cheque was not paid until those cheques had gone into the account. But those cheques did not provide the wages : those cheques reduced the overdraft ; and the wages cheque was paid by money which was advanced by the bank for the purpose. And that is shown in the clearest terms in the form of the account."

The decision was accordingly in favour of the bank, but it illustrates the point that in cases of this kind, where you do not wish the debit balance to go over a certain maximum, you should not use words which may be construed against you and to your disadvantage. Do not say or write anything about paying in to meet any withdrawals at all, because, if you do, you may thereby unwittingly make a specific appropriation. In Whatmough's case, to which we shall come shortly, the instruction which had been given was, not to issue any further cheques without providing the necessary funds. Now that just exactly meant specific appropriation of the new lodgments as against the new withdrawals, thereby leaving the previous old debit just where it was—probably not the result intended by the bank at all. Rather say to your customer in cases of this kind to carry on with his operations, but not to let the balance on the account get any larger. I shall go into this important matter from the practical point of view in a subsequent lecture.

What saved the bank in Freedman's case was (*first*) while they paid out cash in respect of the cheques paid in, they protected the position by taking a wages cheque from the customers ; they could quite well have paid out the cash for the cheques presented for payment without taking a wages cheque, but, if they had done that, they would have had no claim whatever ; and (*second*) the customer's account in the ledger and presumably also the pass book were properly kept, showing without any break or interruption in the account the cheques paid in on the one side and the wages cheques paid out on the other.

Had the loose conversations referred to by the Judge been incorporated or confirmed in letters either to or from the bank they would probably have had a poor case, and if they had opened a new or separate account to be kept at credit in respect of the wages they would have been quite unsuccessful in their claim for a preferential ranking.

You will appreciate that, owing to the making out of the wages cheques and the continuation of the original current account without any break or interruption, the rule in Clayton's case operated very advantageously to the National Provincial Bank, in that all the weekly lodgments went to extinguish the earliest unpaid items on the debit side for which the bank probably held no security and certainly had no preference while the weekly payments on the wages cheques were running up an entirely new debt for which the bank were entitled to a preference under the Companies Act. The more a thing like that goes on, the better always for the bank.

Prior to your debtor customer being made legally bankrupt—that is, while he is insolvent and unable to pay his due debts *on demand*—there are certain transactions into which it is not safe for any of his creditors to enter with him because, as the law stands, these transactions are reducible later on at the instance of the trustee on his sequestrated estate involving, it may be, the handing back of money received in payment of a debt or the giving up of some security taken against it. This is a position which you should endeavour to avoid, and you will be able to do so through your knowledge of what I have already said and what I am about to say to you and by your paying attention to your position at the time.

Our common law strikes at all acts of fraud on the part of any debtor whereby he endeavours, to the prejudice and at the expense of his creditors, to provide for himself or his relatives or to favour particularly any one of his creditors more than the others.

Gratuitous alienations by any bankrupt are struck at by the common law which prevents him from making gifts or putting away his estate out of the reach of his creditors at a time when he is insolvent. Such transactions are open to reduction at the instance of the trustee on the bankrupt's estate, and, in order to achieve success, all the trustee has to do is to show that there was no real consideration received by the bankrupt for the transaction and that he was insolvent at the time.

Fraudulent preferences given by a bankrupt to any of his creditors to the exclusion or prejudice of the others are also struck at by common law, and you must therefore always take care in your dealings with a debtor customer that you do nothing, in recovering payment of your debt, which the Court might hold to be tainted with fraud and therefore reducible. Whatmough's case is an example of an attempt made to saddle a bank with participation in a simulate or fraudulent transaction to secure payment of their own debt in full to the disadvantage of the other creditors.

In 1621 it was found that the evils arising from fraudulent transactions of the kind referred to were so great that the Scots Parliament passed an Act dealing with gratuitous alienations to conjunct and confident persons, and later on, in 1696, they passed another Act dealing with the position in a more masterly way for the protection of the general body of creditors, and rendered it unnecessary to make any averment of fraud or insolvency before the objectionable transactions could be reduced.

The Act of 1696 declares to be void and null all and whatsoever voluntary dispositions, assignations or other deeds which shall be found to be made or granted directly or indirectly by the debtor either at or within sixty days before his bankruptcy in favour of any of his creditors either for their satisfaction or further security in preference to his other creditors.

Sec. 4 of the Bankruptcy (Scotland) Act, 1913, provides that the date of a deed under that Act or under the Act of 1696 is the date of registration or intimation thereof—not merely the date when the deed in question was signed.

Accordingly any security granted at any time in respect of a past due debt is reducible unless it has been completed by being recorded or intimated in the usual way more than sixty days prior to the date of the granter's notour bankruptcy.

Any voluntary act on the part of a debtor within the sixty days whereby any of his creditors receive satisfaction—that is, something different from a cash payment as you will see later—or security for a debt previously existing will therefore be cut down without the necessity of averring that the debtor was guilty of fraud or was even insolvent. These points are made irrelevant, and the only question is whether the transaction took place within the sixty days.

There are, however, three well-known exceptions to the Act. They are not contained in the Act, but have been evolved out of a long series of decisions in the Courts regarding transactions of the nature in question. These exceptions are :—

1. *Nova debita*—that is, new transactions.— There is nothing to prevent a debtor from entering into a new transaction within the sixty days such as borrowing money and giving a security therefor at the time. He may purchase goods from you and pay your account therefor within the period, and so on. If you lend your customer money and are unable to get from him at the moment a security therefor, you can take from him an obligation to give you a security for that loan, and provided that the security is specific and the obligation to give it is definite in point of time, your position will be good even although the security is not actually granted or completed until within the sixty days. If, however, the obligation to give you such a security is not specific as to the security subjects, or is not definite in point of time, your security will be bad because the granting of the security will then be a voluntary act on the part of your customer and so struck at by the Statute.

If, as sometimes happens in a case of this kind, your customer hands you scrip for some investment or the titles of his house with an undertaking to give you a valid security thereon whenever called upon, then such deposit and undertaking will be of no use to you unless you have actually completed your security before the sixty days begin to run. To be effectual the undertaking ought to be to the effect that your customer will give you a security over the asset in question forthwith—not merely when called on—and you should not delay in getting and completing the security so undertaken to be given.

2. The Act, it has been held, does not strike at the payment in cash by the debtor of any of his outstanding debts whether incurred prior or subsequent to the commencement of the sixty days. Cash in this connection does not mean legal tender, but includes payment by cheque, or by bill, draft, post office order, &c.

While a valid cash payment may thus be made by cheque, it must be the debtor's own cheque. Such a cheque relates to the debtor's own cash in the hands of his own banker, and is therefore, in law, the equivalent of the debtor's own cash. It will not do for him, however, to hand to his creditor an indorsed cheque which he has received drawn in his favour. Such an indorsed cheque does not relate to the debtor's own cash at all and is nothing more or less than an assignation of funds belonging to a third party. The case of *Carter* v. *Johnstone* (1886, 13 R. 698) is an illustration of this. There a man within the sixty days preceding his bankruptcy had indorsed a cheque on which he was the payee and handed it

128

to one of his creditors in payment of a past due debt. The Court of Session held that such indorsement and delivery of the cheque were reducible under the Act of 1696 as being neither a cash payment nor a transaction in the ordinary course of business. You might keep this case particularly in mind as I intend to refer to it again when we come to Whatmough's case.

3. The remaining class of transactions excepted from the 1696 Act are what are termed transactions in the ordinary course of business, but there is nothing anywhere to show whether one is to look at the ordinary course of the creditor's business or the ordinary course of the debtor's business. If there is any regular series of dealings between any two parties, I think one would have regard to what was the ordinary course of dealing between these two. If, however, it were one isolated transaction it is a little difficult to know what standard of ordinary course of business one could apply.

In *Carter* v. *Johnstone* just mentioned, the Court held that the indorsement of a cheque to a creditor was not in the ordinary course of business engaged in by the parties in question, but it is just possible to imagine a case of a debtor who had no bank account of his own and regularly paid his tradesmen's bills by means of indorsed cheques on which he is the payee. Generally speaking, however, any transaction which is out of the usual run and not recognised as a standard method in the settlement of debts will be struck at.

Newton's Trustee v. *Finlayson & Co. Ltd.* (1928, S.C. 637) was a case where a firm of builders were engaged in work on a church, the contract price being payable by instalments. The firm were at that time insolvent, and arrestments were lodged by two of their creditors in the hands of the Church Trustees to attach an instalment then due. The firm wrote to these Trustees requesting that payment of that instalment should be made to the arresting creditors, whose solicitors also wrote to the Trustees agreeing to the withdrawal of the arrestment on the footing that payment of that instalment was made to them. The money was accordingly paid by the Church Trustees to the creditors' law agents in terms of this arrangement, and at a meeting between the insolvent firm, the law agents, and one of the arresting creditors the law agents produced the sum of £275 in bank notes, and, after some discussion, the creditor received £200 in cash and the insolvent firm received the remaining £75. The estates of the firm were sequestrated within sixty days thereafter.

The trustee in the sequestration, having brought an action against the creditor for repayment of that £200, as being an illegal preference at common law and also under the 1696 Act, the Court held that the receipt of the £200 by the creditor was a simulate cash transaction; that the debtors' request to the Church Trustees to pay the instalment to the arresting creditors, although granted in consideration of the withdrawal of the arrestment, was a voluntary deed on the part of the debtors; that it was not a payment in cash although it was cash that the creditor actually got, but a transfer of a debt due to the bankrupts; and that, accordingly, the transaction was reducible as an illegal preference under the Act in consequence of which the creditor had to hand the £200 back to the trustee and take an ordinary ranking therefor in the sequestration.

Attention may also be drawn to the case *John* v. *Mendoza*, decided on 24th October 1938. In this case the plaintiff, on receiving a written acknowledgment of the debt, refrained from proving in the bankruptcy of the defendant. The bankruptcy order was subsequently annulled on the ground that all the debts were paid in full, and it was held that the plaintiff could not recover thereafter by action a debt for which he could and should have proved in the bankruptcy.

There is just one other case I should like to bring before you in connection with a fraudulent preference in bankruptcy before we pass on to Whatmough's case. This case is *Lyons Trustee* v. *Barclays Bank Ltd.*—also known as *in re* Lyons— (51 T.L.R. 24).

Lyons, the debtor, was a customer of Barclays Bank and had an overdraft with them to the extent of £2000, which was secured by a guarantee for that amount given to the bank by the debtor's father.

The debtor having become insolvent, and knowing that he could not pay twenty shillings in the £, stopped making payments to the general body of his creditors and proceeded to pay to the credit of his bank account all the moneys which he could collect from his business debtors, by means of which the overdraft account was reduced from the £2000 to somewhere in the region of £1300, and as a direct consequence of which the father's liability under his guarantee was similarly reduced. In other words, the father benefited by his son's actings to the extent of the lodgments—about

£700. There was, however, no evidence that any pressure had been brought to bear on the debtor to do this either by the father or by the bank.

The debtor's bankruptcy ensued within the period prescribed by the English Bankruptcy Act, and the father settled his liability to the bank under his guarantee by paying up the outstanding balance of £1300 which, of course, squared the account.

The trustee on the bankrupt estate then sued Barclays and also the guarantor for payment of the £700 collected by the debtor and deliberately applied in reduction of his overdraft for the benefit of the bank and of the guarantor in preference to, and to the prejudice of, the other creditors.

Mr Justice Clauson, who tried the case, said that the fair inference to be drawn from the facts was that, in not closing down his business but trying to carry it on and paying to the bank the moneys collected from his business debtors, the bankrupt was acting with the dominant intention of relieving his father of his liability under his guarantee—in other words, preferring his father before his other creditors within the meaning of the Act. The result was that the lodgments of about £700 were held to be fraudulent and void, and the bank were ordered to repay that amount to the trustee.

There was a side-issue in that case as to the right of the bank to recover that £700 from the guarantor because obviously he had paid £700 too little under his guarantee, but it was held that the bank could not recover.

This decision of Mr Justice Clauson was, however, reversed on appeal later, apparently on the ground that the trustee on the bankrupt's estate had failed to show a definite intention on the part of the bankrupt to benefit any one creditor in preference to another.

We now come to *Whatmough's Trustee* v. *The British Linen Bank* (1934, S.C. H.L. 51). Harold Whatmough, a customer of the British Linen Bank at Gourock, had carried on business as a motor-bus proprietor for a number of years. His account with the bank was overdrawn and as a matter of fact he was insolvent. After protracted negotiations, he arranged a sale of his business and assets to the L.M.S. Railway Company at the price of £20,000 on condition that he cleared off the remaining liability on his buses which he held under hire purchase agreements.

The price of the business was paid to Whatmough's solicitor, who, in terms of the bargain, paid off the balance of the hire purchase instalments, but when that had been done there was not sufficient money left to pay all the creditors in full.

The bank had been pressing for repayment of the overdraft for some time previously, and Whatmough had apparently given their agent a promise that he would have that done when the settlement of the price of the business had taken place. Whatmough accordingly went to his solicitor and obtained from him a cheque for £7300 out of the balance of the price still in hand. This cheque, which was on the solicitor's current account with the Union Bank, was drawn payable to Whatmough and was, with some other small amounts which he had available, just sufficient to square the overdraft. He took this cheque to his bankers, the British Linen, indorsed it, and paid it in to the credit of the account, which was then closed and the securities pledged by his wife therefor released.

Whatmough having been made bankrupt almost immediately afterwards, the trustee raised an action against the bank for repayment of the £7300. The grounds of the trustee's claim were that the transaction did not fall under any of the exceptions from the Act and that it was, therefore, struck at by the Act, and that in any case if not struck at by the Act, it was struck at by the common law as a fraudulent transaction. He pleaded :—

1. That this was not a payment of a debt in cash, and founded upon the decisions in *Carter* v. *Johnstone* and *Blincow* v. *Allan's Trustees* (1833, 7 W. & S. 26) and other similar cases where payments made by means of indorsed bills and cheques had been held not to be payments in cash.

2. That this was not a transaction in the ordinary course of business, because operations on the bank account had ceased about three months before, and that the relationship which latterly existed between the bank and Whatmough was no longer that of banker and customer, but merely that of creditor and debtor ; and

3. That in any case the transaction was struck at by common law because of collusion in that the bank had insisted upon payment of their debt being made in full out of a fund which was insufficient to meet the claims of all the creditors.

The Lord Ordinary (Mackay) granted decree in favour of the trustee. On appeal the Inner House unanimously granted decree in favour of the bank, and the House of Lords also unanimously decided in favour of the bank. That meant that the whole nine judges of the appellate Courts were unanimously of opinion that the tenth judge—the Lord Ordinary—was wrong, and in these circumstances there would not seem to be much more to be said on the subject. It will do no harm, however, to look at the matter somewhat more closely and give a little consideration to the reasoning on which the House of Lords arrived at that decision.

I need not trouble you with the opinions of the various judges as to the trustee's pleas as to fraudulent preference and transaction out of the ordinary course of business. There was no unanimity on these points which, however, did not form the basis of the decision ultimately arrived at.

The trustee's other plea was that this was not a cash transaction, but nine out of the ten judges held that it was, although not all for the same reason. The net result on this aspect of the case may be summed up in the words of Lord Thankerton, who gave the leading opinion in the House of Lords. In the course of his discussion of the case from the point of view of a cash transaction he said :—

" It is necessary in the first place to determine whether the bank held the cheque for £7300 as agents for collection or as holders for value, or in other words whether on clearance they received payment of the cheque for their customer or for themselves. . . . I am, therefore, of opinion that the cheque for £7300 was handed to the bank for collection by them as agents for the debtor, on the footing that the proceeds of the cheque when paid should be applied by the bank in reduction of the overdraft."

135

On that reasoning the decision was that the bank should succeed because it was a cash transaction.

This is a point to which I would like you to pay particular attention. The handing over of the indorsed cheque across the counter is tacitly admitted not to be cash—the bank's debt was not paid off by that. But when the bank as collecting agents cleared the cheque they then received cash or its legal equivalent from the paying banker, and with that cash they, as collecting agents for their customer, paid off the debt due by him to them as previously arranged. This involves, of course, the admission that, if the handing over of the cheque across the counter had itself been payment, or if the bank had taken the cheque as holders for value, it would not have been a cash transaction—that is what *Carter* v. *Johnstone* laid down.

Now, to my mind the decision in this case rests, and rests solely, upon the answer to this question : did the bank take that cheque as agents for collection, as Lord Thankerton said ? If so, then it probably was a cash transaction. Or, on the other hand, did they take the cheque in any other capacity, such as holders for value ? In the latter event it was not a cash transaction.

Let us see whether we can find the answer to that question. Let us take the following excerpt from the evidence led while the bank's Gourock agent was in the box giving evidence. This is what passed on this subject :—

> (*Q*) Supposing Mr Agnew (the drawer of the cheque in question) had died before you got the money from the bank on which the cheque was drawn, what would your position have been ?

(*A*) You mean if the cheque had been returned " drawer deceased " ?

(*Q*) Yes.

(*A*) The position would be that we would have to advise the customer (Whatmough) and then we could take recourse against the payee and drawer.

(*Q*) On the cheque ?

(*A*) Yes.

(*Q*) You would sue on the cheque in that event ?

(*A*) Yes.

That does not look as if the bank were mere agents for collection. An agent for collection, as you know, cannot sue the drawer of an unpaid cheque, and it seems clear that the bank held and gave evidence that they held the cheque as holders for value. Lord Thankerton, however, did not agree that the bank were holders for value, as their own agent had asserted at the proof, and dismissed the evidence given by the bank's agent by saying—

> It is true that Mr Stewart (the bank agent) states that the bank on the amount being credited to the debtor in their books would be in the position of holders for value, but that erroneous view does not assist the appellant, Whatmough's trustee.

Now, was that an erroneous view ? Was the bank agent wrong in saying that he was a holder for value and that he was not an agent for collection ? Test this for yourselves by asking yourselves the following simple question :—

> Assume that Whatmough had returned to the bank again a few moments after handing in the cheque and said to the agent, " I have

changed my mind about that cheque. I
don't want you to act as my agent in its
collection. Your authority from me to act
as such agent for collection is cancelled.
Give me back the cheque which is still my
property." Would the bank agent have
handed the cheque back or would he not ?

I think there is only one answer to that question,
but if I am wrong, if anyone should think there
may be another answer possible, then let me
draw your attention to something which, curiously
enough, does not appear from the reports to have
been read to the House of Lords. It is sec. 27 (3)
of the Bills of Exchange Act of 1882. It says—

> Where the holder of a bill has a lien on it
> arising either from contract or by implication
> of law he is deemed to be a holder for value
> to the extent of the sum for which he has
> a lien.

Surely that puts the answer to the question
beyond all doubt. If it does, then this important
case would appear to have been wrongly decided,
but, right or wrong, we must for the time being
accept it as it stands.

Now if that had been the end of the matter
things might not have been so bad and bankers
and trustees in bankruptcy might have been able
to struggle along not so badly in the future, but,
unfortunately, the fact is that that is not the end
of the matter.

Superficially one would say that it was a good
decision from the point of view of the banks in
that it gave them an assured position for the
future as regards the lodgment of indorsed cheques
by a customer within sixty days of his bankruptcy.

Well, it does that, but only until such time as some other trustee in bankruptcy raises the same question, as he is perfectly entitled to do and probably will do, if he has a bankruptcy where the conditions are right and the sum at stake sufficiently large to tempt him to test the question.

Apart from all that, however, there is still another aspect of the case which cannot be ignored. I used to think that, notwithstanding the somewhat conflicting decisions of the past, it was not a difficult task in any given case where a bank received from a customer an indorsed cheque across the counter to determine whether that bank was a holder for value or merely an agent for collection, but this decision of Whatmoughs, by which we must now all meantime be bound, has rather upset the previous generally accepted ideas.

Usually a banker with an overdrawn account, when he did not need any protection under sec. 82 of the 1882 Act against a claim by a true owner, would take up the attitude that he was a holder for value because his customer was indebted to him on his current account, and he would successfully assert his right to demand and receive payment from the drawer of the cheque. That undoubtedly has been the law hitherto.

Now, however, the House of Lords have apparently said that he cannot do that because he cannot be a holder for value. Whatmough was deeply indebted to the British Linen Bank when he handed the cheque across the counter ; that bank had a lien on the cheque ; there was no question about a forged indorsement on it ; the protection of sec. 82 against a true owner was not required by the bank—in short, there could have been no clearer case for a claim to be a holder for value, and the bank's own agent asserted in the evidence I quoted to you that that was his position—he claimed to be a holder for value and would have sued the drawer of the cheque if it had been returned unpaid. The House of Lords have definitely said, however, that that view is erroneous.

Lord Macmillan in the course of his opinion said—There are, no doubt, exceptional cases where the bank becomes itself the holder of the cheque for its own behoof, but, in the present case, there is nothing to show that the transaction between the bankrupt and his bank with reference to the cheque in question took place otherwise than in conformity with the usual course of business where a customer pays in a cheque of which he is the payee.

If that is so, and if in the usual course of business it is only as agent for collection that a bank takes in such an indorsed cheque, it is almost impossible to see when the exceptional cases referred to by Lord Macmillan could arise where the bank becomes itself the holder for value.

LECTURE II.

In the previous lecture I dealt with the law relating to a variety of circumstances connected with insolvency generally and with what one might term the antecedents of legal bankruptcy, and now I wish to deal more particularly with the immediate consequences of sequestration so far as bankers are concerned.

Perhaps before doing so, however, it might be well if I were to give you a short outline of the formal procedure connected with an award of sequestration, but, as you are not so very deeply interested in this, I will make the outline as short and as simple as possible.

When any debtor's financial position has become acute, he may be relieved of all his debts and obligations by sequestration of his estates in terms of the Bankruptcy (Scotland) Act, 1913, under which all his assets are taken and realised and the proceeds distributed among his various creditors according to their respective rights and interests.

This end may be achieved by the debtor himself, with the concurrence of one or more creditors whose debts together amount to not less than £50, petitioning the Court for sequestration of his estates. He, however, requires no concurrence of creditors in the case of a summary sequestration —that is, where his assets do not exceed £300.

141

On the other hand, any creditor of his who holds a decree against him, on which the period of the charge for payment has expired, may apply for sequestration of the debtor's estate, but, if his debt does not amount to £50, he requires the concurrence of other creditors with debts amounting to at least that sum. In the case of a summary sequestration the debt must exceed £10.

It is not competent for a creditor to petition for sequestration of his debtor's estates unless the debtor be notour bankrupt, that is, unless the petitioning creditor, or some other creditor, holds a decree of the Court or something equivalent on which the days of charge are expired. It is not sufficient if the creditors have merely accounts or debts due to them not constituted by decree. The debtor must first of all be made notour bankrupt by a decree of the Court followed by an expired charge thereon.

In the case of a petition for sequestration being presented to the Court by a duly qualified creditor, it is first of all served upon the debtor and advertised in the *Edinburgh Gazette,* and, if no steps are taken to oppose the application, the Court pronounces an award of sequestration and fixes a date for the first meeting of the creditors at which the election of the trustee and commissioners takes place. On the result of that meeting being reported to the Court, the trustee, assuming that there is no dispute as to his appointment, finds caution for his intromissions to an extent specified by the creditors, and the formal act and warrant in his favour is then issued, and this forms his judicial title to the bankrupt's estate.

The trustee's act and warrant may not be granted by the Court for some weeks after the presentation of the petition because the bankrupt may have entered appearance to endeavour to stop the proceedings, or there may have been a dispute as to which of two competing parties nominated as trustee has been validly elected. When it is granted, however, the act and warrant draws back to the date of the first deliverance on the petition, which is regarded as the actual date of the commencement of the sequestration.

The act and warrant has the legal effect of transferring to and vesting in the trustee for behoof of the creditors absolutely and irredeemably the whole property of the bankrupt of every kind and wherever situated and all his right, title and interest therein. The trustee, however, takes the estate *tantum et tale* as vested in the bankrupt at the date of the sequestration and subject to the legal rights of third parties therein and subject to certain exceptions.

The bankrupt's clothing and tools of trade, for example, do not fall under the sequestration. If he is entitled to any alimentary liferent or annuity under a will or marriage contract it will not fall under the sequestration except to the extent which the Court may think to be in excess of what he reasonably requires for his maintenance, but any contingent or future rights, such as legacies and so on, not yet vested under a will or marriage contract or other deed of an irrevocable nature fall within the sequestration.

The English Bankruptcy Act of 1914, generally speaking, achieves the same result in the long-run as our Bankruptcy Act of 1913 coupled with our old Acts of 1621 and 1696 and, of course, our common law. The method in England of achieving the object is somewhat different from that employed by us. The question does not really affect you to any extent, but I have been asked to say a word or two on the subject.

Under sec. 37 of the English Bankruptcy Act, the bankruptcy is deemed to have relation back to, and to commence at the time of, what is called the act of bankruptcy committed by the debtor. This act of bankruptcy is defined as meaning any one or more of certain things done by a debtor in relation to his affairs. For example, it is an act of bankruptcy for any debtor to make a fraudulent conveyance or gift of his property. This may have taken place some time before the bankruptcy proceedings are commenced, but, when they are commenced, they draw back to the date of that act of bankruptcy and not, as is the case with us here, merely to the date of the first deliverance. In this way all the transactions of the bankrupt subsequent to that act of bankruptcy are open to criticism and challenge by the trustee, but to this there are exceptions, very much the same as we have to the 1696 Act, by way of *nova debita*, cash transactions, and transactions in the ordinary course of business. The result of it all in the end, however, is more or less the same as we have here.

Having been made bankrupt, and so long as he has not received a discharge from the Court, the debtor is no longer able to acquire and hold assets in his own right, although he may take or continue in a situation at a salary or even carry on business on his own account. The Trustee, however, is entitled to get from him, if he does so, any salary or profits in excess of what may reasonably be required for the suitable maintenance of himself and his dependants. One thing he must not do is to incur any new debt exceeding

£10 without disclosing that he is an undischarged bankrupt—that is a punishable offence.

The next step is the examination of the bankrupt, which takes place in Court, when he may be subjected to an inquisition as to his position and his assets and transactions and the circumstances which rendered him unable to pay his debts. The trustee has the right to have any of the bankrupt's relatives or friends or even third parties subjected to a similar examination in Court if he thinks that he may thereby obtain any necessary or desirable information as to the bankrupt's assets and transactions.

Without resorting to sequestration, however, an insolvent person's estates may be wound up by a private arrangement with his creditors. This usually takes the form of a trust deed for behoof of the creditors. Such a trust deed is, of course, granted voluntarily and contains a conveyance by the debtor to the trustee of his whole assets, but the trustee has no statutory title and therefore must complete his right to the subjects conveyed in the usual way by intimation, registration, infeftment and so on. A trust deed, however, relates only to the estate actually belonging to the debtor at the time, and does not cover or convey to the trustee any future or contingent assets as in the case of a sequestration.

A trust deed for creditors usually contains express provisions for all the creditors being ranked and preferred on the estate in accordance with their legal rights and preferences just as if it were a sequestration, and also for the acceptance by the creditors of any dividend which may be paid by the trustee in full and final settlement of their claims. There is no formal examination of the bankrupt or of third parties under a trust deed, but the bankrupt usually attends the first meeting of the creditors to give any explanations they may require as to his affairs. There are no restrictions under a trust deed against the bankrupt retaining after-acquired assets, and he does not require to give up any part of his future salary or profits to the creditors. Once all the creditors accede to the trust deed the bankrupt is discharged, and, unlike the bankrupt in a sequestration, he is free to accumulate a new estate to which these creditors have no right. If any of the creditors, however, are not satisfied that the bankrupt should be in this favourable position they usually either refuse to accede to the trust deed or insist upon sequestration being taken out.

As the procedure under a trust deed is entirely voluntary, no creditor is bound to accede or agree to the debtor's assets and liabilities being dealt with in that way. Every creditor is entitled, without acceding to the trust deed, to rank on the estate and draw a dividend *pari passu* with every other creditor and without the necessity of valuing and deducting any securities which he may hold, and he may still sue later on for any balance not so recovered. Of course, if the creditor accedes to the trust deed, he is bound by its terms, which, as I have said, will put him in the same position as if it were a sequestration. Where any creditor refuses to accede to the trust deed and insists on his right to claim a *pari passu* ranking without deducting his securities, the other creditors will naturally enforce the alternative under a sequestration and thereby compel that non-acceding creditor to fall into line.

A limited company cannot be sequestrated and cannot grant a trust deed for behoof of its creditors, but the same result is achieved by the appointment of a liquidator, and this may be done either on a resolution of the company itself to wind up or by the Court ordering the company to be wound up and appointing a liquidator on an application at the instance of any of the creditors.

If a creditor to the extent of £50 or upwards wishes to have a debtor limited company wound up it is not necessary that he should raise an action in Court and obtain a decree, as must be done in the case of sequestration of an individual. All a creditor has to do in the case of a limited company is to send to the company a formal demand, in accordance with sec. 169 of the Companies Act of 1929, for payment of his debt, and, if it is not paid within twenty-one days thereafter, he can then apply to the Court for liquidation without any further formality.

This is a very valuable provision in the interests of creditors of a limited company and puts such creditors in a much more favourable position than the creditors of an individual, who have first of all to raise an action in Court for their debt, where they may be met with all sorts of delays owing to continuations being granted and dilatory defences being put forward and all the other evils of litigation before they obtain the necessary decree. That need not happen in the case of a limited company.

The date of the commencement of the winding up of a limited company, which is the important date for you, is the date when the company passed the resolution to go into liquidation, or, in the case of a compulsory liquidation, the date of the presentment of the petition to the Court.

The Companies Act of 1929, which now regulates all limited companies, incorporates various sections of the Bankruptcy Act, the result being that a liquidator in the winding up of a limited company and a trustee on the sequestrated estates of an individual are more or less in the same general position with regard to the assets of the company or of the individual and the rights and powers of realisation, administration and distribution thereof. There are, of course, certain technical differences between the two, but they are not of sufficient importance in the present connection to warrant my spending time explaining them to you in detail.

As there is, for all practical purposes, no essential difference between the winding up of the affairs of a company and the winding up of the affairs of an individual, whether under sequestration or under a trust deed, with the few exceptions just referred to, I propose in this lecture to deal with the banker's position as if his customer were an individual whose estates were being dealt with under a process of sequestration.

Assuming, therefore, that the customer's bankruptcy is now an accomplished fact, whether by way of sequestration, trust deed, or liquidation, what the banker has to do is to make the most of the unfortunate position in which he finds himself. The first step is to prepare and lodge the usual affidavit and claim.

Before you do that, however, you should, where it is a case of a trust deed for creditors, obtain first of all the consent of any guarantor you may have or any third party pledgor, as you are not entitled voluntarily to let your debtor off for less than the full amount of the debt and then expect the guarantor or third party pledgor to pay up the balance. Although your documents may authorise you to accede to trust deeds or compound with your debtors it is not always safe to rely on these as they may not help you in the particular circumstances. Such consent is not required, however, in the case of sequestrations or liquidations.

The affidavit and claim is normally made up by Head Office as the affidavit should be sworn by one of the principal officers of the bank, but, generally speaking, no objection is taken to the validity of the claim in cases where it is signed by the agent at the branch where the customer's account was kept. This point really only arises where there is a competition for the trusteeship, as each candidate carefully scrutinises the affidavits and claims lodged by his opponent and states his objections to the validity thereof before the Court if he thinks he can thereby cut down the support and votes on which his opponent is relying to get him the appointment. If, therefore, you wish any nominee of yours to be appointed Trustee, it is necessary that your affidavit and claim be signed by one of the bank's principal officers and not by one of their agents. If, however, you are not really interested in who gets the appointment there is nothing to prevent the agent signing the claim, as the trustee, once he is appointed, usually accepts this without question.

In preparing the affidavit and claim you require to set forth your customer's whole position with you and produce the vouchers or documents of debt on which your claim is based. The actual amount of your claim must be stated with interest thereon, down to the date of the commencement of the bankruptcy, and, on the other hand, if you are claiming in respect of a debt not yet due, such as a bill at a currency, you must deduct from its amount the interest applicable to the period subsequent to the date of the bankruptcy.

As regards this matter of interest you must not be misled by the terms of a cash credit bond and disposition in security if you happen to hold anything of that kind. That document, as you know, provides security over the property pledged up to a specified sum of principal with three years' interest thereon at 5 per cent. If it happens that your advances exceed that principal sum or that the interest is more than three years in arrear, you are nevertheless entitled to claim for the full sum due to you, and all the interest outstanding no matter for what period, not only against the bankrupt estate, but also against any guarantor or other co-obligant for the debt. The only limitation on your right under such a cash credit bond is that you cannot take out of the security subjects themselves anything more than the specified principal sum and three years' interest thereon. If you do, you must hand the excess back to the trustee as part of the bankrupt's estate or to a postponed security holder if there should be one. But that does not affect your claim against the bankrupt's estate for a ranking for your full debt and all the arrears of interest outstanding, no matter for what period, nor your claim against a guarantor or third party pledgor.

There are various classes of debts which may be due by a bankrupt in respect of which some one or other of his creditors may be entitled to a preference over the others. Such preference may, for example, be for wages unpaid, rates and taxes outstanding and so on, but, so far as a banker is concerned, there is only one thing for which he can claim a preference.

The Companies Act of 1929 made a change in the law which is of considerable benefit to bankers, and which does not appear to be too well known to all those directly interested in the matter. There are certain technical difficulties in working out the banker's rights, and the following observations may be of assistance in securing full advantage of the position.

Sec. 264 (1) provides that in the winding up of a limited company there shall be paid in priority to all other debts of the company certain rates, taxes and other charges, and also (*a*) all wages or salary (including commission) not exceeding £50 of any clerk or servant in respect of services rendered to the company during the four months preceding the date of the winding up order, in the case of a company ordered to be wound up compulsorily which had not previously commenced to be wound up voluntarily, and in any other case the date of the commencement of the winding up ; and (*b*) all wages of any workman or labourer not exceeding £25, whether payable for time or for piecework, in respect of services rendered to the company during two months preceding the same date.

Subsec. (3) of that section provides that where any payment on account of wages or salary has been made to any clerk, servant, workman or labourer in the employment of a company out of money advanced by some person for that purpose, that person shall, in a winding up, have a right of priority in respect of the money so advanced and paid up to the amount by which the sum in respect of which that clerk, servant, workman or labourer would have been entitled to priority in the winding up has been diminished by reason of the payment having been made.

Quite frequently advances to meet wages are made by a bank to a limited company in a difficult financial position, and this subsection gives a measure of protection in respect of these advances over and above any securities which may be held for the company's obligations. In fact, where a guarantee has been given or securities pledged by a third party it is the duty of the bank to take as full advantage as possible of the preferential claim so as to minimise such third party loss.

It will be noticed, however, that the benefit conferred by subsec. (3) is subject to certain conditions which require to be complied with. The money must be advanced " for that purpose " —that is, for the purpose of paying wages or salaries—and it is accordingly necessary to preserve evidence that the advances in question were so made. The simplest method of doing that is to have the cheques which are drawn for the purpose specially marked by the customers as being for wages. They may, for example, be made payable to " Selves for Wages " or " Wages or bearer." It is not sufficient if the cheques have merely a marking on the back to show the numbers and denominations of the notes and coins drawn from the bank or that the banker assumed or understood that the money was required to meet wages. The money, according to the Act, must have been advanced for the specific purpose, and this involves definiteness.

Again, the preference is only given in so far as the employees' priority claims in the liquidation have been diminished by reason of the advances in question having been made. If the money, although specially borrowed for the purpose, is not actually applied in paying the wages, the position would be that the employees' claims in the liquidation would not have been diminished and they themselves would be entitled to a preferential ranking in full. Consequently the bank in a case of that kind could not also obtain a preferential ranking and would require to be satisfied with an ordinary ranking. No doubt, however, any director or officer of the company who obtained advances from a bank for the specific purpose of paying wages, and instead of doing so applied the money otherwise, would lay himself open to a charge of fraud.

It is in the general case impossible for any bank to be certain that money borrowed from them in this way is actually or wholly required to meet wages falling within the Act or that it will be applied wholly for that purpose. All that can be done from the practical point of view is to be reasonably assured of the correctness of the amount of each payment in view of the number of employees understood to be working and to trust to the integrity of the company's officials for the rest.

It is thought better to debit cheques for wages advanced to the company's general account and not to a special wages account, because it would be possible for the company at the last moment to appropriate a lodgment to the credit of the wages account and thus defeat the expected preference therefor. It would, of course, be open to the bank, if they thought it best to have a special account for these advances, to take a letter from the company agreeing that they would not appropriate lodgments to the credit of that account without the consent of the bank, but that ought to be done at the opening of the account and not at the last moment.

In the event of the company going into liquidation, it is necessary for the bank to make up the usual affidavit and claim in order to obtain the preferential ranking to which they ought to be entitled. This affidavit and claim will state the total amount of the bank's claim, and will include a claim for a preferential ranking in respect of the sums advanced for the payment of wages.

As an illustration of the method of making up such a preferential claim for advances in respect of wages, a case may be taken where these have been debited to the company's general account which, at the date of the liquidation, shows a debit balance of, say, £3450. That sum is made up of the latest debits to the account which total up to that figure. A summation, therefore, requires to be made backwards from the last entry until a total figure of £3450 is reached. A line drawn at that point in the column will show exactly all the various advances still outstanding— all others having, in accordance with the rule in Clayton's case, been repaid by the credits on the other side. The details of the current account in the bank's ledger may be assumed to be as follows :—

1933			Debits.	Credits.	Balance.
Aug.	1.	Balance at date £1543			*Dr.* £1543
,,	2.			£157	*Dr.* 1386
,,	3.		220		*Dr.* 1606
,,	5.			595	*Dr.* 1011
,,	7.			729	*Dr.* 282
,,	10.		1150		*Dr.* 1432
,,	14.			811	*Dr.* 621
,,	17.			378	*Dr.* 243
,,	31.	Wages 100			*Dr.* 343
Sept.	12.			243	*Dr.* 100
,,	15.		567		*Dr.* 667
,,	20.		310		*Dr.* 977
,,	30.	Wages 100			*Dr.* 1077
Oct.	10.		396		*Dr.* 1473
,,	17.		420		*Dr.* 1893
,,	31.	Wages 100			*Dr.* 1993
Nov.	11.		429		*Dr.* 2422
,,	21.		511		*Dr.* 2933
,,	30.	Wages 100			*Dr.* 3033
Dec.	20.		317		*Dr.* 3350
,,	31.	Wages 100			*Dr.* 3450
			£6363	£2913	

Debit Balance, £3450.   Liquidation date, 15th January 1934.

Summing these debit items backwards the amount of the outstanding debit balance of £3450 is reached at 31st August 1933, so that the item of £1150 on 10th August has been repaid as well as all previous debits.

In selecting the advances which are entitled to a preference, the item of £100 on 31st August must be omitted as it is outside the four months' limit.

The remaining four items of £100 each must now be analysed, and the proportion thereof applicable to workmen and labourers on the one hand and clerks and servants on the other ascertained. Assume that the result is :—

Month.	Clerks.	Workmen.
Sept.	£30	£70
Oct.	30	70
Nov.	30	70
Dec.	30	70
	£120	£280

This shows that the workmen's wages within the two months preceding the liquidation amounted to £140, and that the remaining £140 of their wages must be omitted from the claim.

On examining the details of the wages further we may find that during the respective periods preceding the liquidation the employees and their total wages were :—

Clerks.		Workmen.	
A. . . .	£60	D. . . .	£30
B. . . .	30	E. . . .	30
C. . . .	30	F. . . .	30
		G. . . .	20
	£120	H. . . .	20
		K. . . .	10
			£140

In this way A.'s claim is in excess of his limit
by £10, and D., E. and F. are in excess of their
limits by £5 each. This involves a further deduction
from the claim of £25.

The result may be summarised thus :—

Total wages advances outstanding		£500
Deduct—		
Wages outside maximum period	£100	
Workmen's wages, do.	140	
Excess clerks' wages	10	
Excess workmen's wages	15	
		265
Net preference claim		£235
Balance for ordinary claim		3215
Total debit balance		£3450

The circumstances will, of course, differ in each
liquidation, but the foregoing will probably furnish
a guide as to the general lines to be followed.

The Bankruptcy (Scotland) Act, 1913, while
providing a preference to the employees of a firm
or individual for wages on similar lines to that
under the Companies Act, does not contain any
corresponding provision for the protection of a
creditor who advances money to a firm or individual
for the purpose of paying wages. Consequently
it is only in the case of a limited company that
there can be such a preferential claim for advances
for that purpose.

The affidavit and claim requires to show the
details of your claim, and this is usually done by
annexing a copy of the last-signed docquet in the
ledger showing the balance at that date together
with a copy of the ledger entries since then bringing
out the balance you now claim to be due at the
date of the bankruptcy.

If you hold any guarantors or co-obligants bound for the debt as well as the bankrupt, these require to be disclosed in the affidavit, and so also do all securities which you hold for the debt whether these securities were given to you by the bankrupt or by a third party. In short, the whole position requires to be disclosed to the trustee.

Now, if any of the securities which you hold were given to you by the bankrupt himself, that really means that so much of your debt, in effect, has already been paid by him and you must accordingly restrict your claim to the balance outstanding after deducting such securities. What you are required to do, therefore, is to place a value on these securities, and, after deducting that value, claim a ranking on the estate in respect of the balance. Each security must be separately valued—you cannot value them all in one cumulo sum.

This valuation of your securities should be as nearly correct as possible because the Bankruptcy Act contains a provision to prevent under-valuation and consequent over-ranking. Sec. 61 gives the trustee a right to call upon you to make over to him for the benefit of the estate any of the bankrupt's securities which you hold, in exchange for the value in cash which you have placed thereon. Consequently, if you put too low a value on your securities, you may be taken advantage of by the trustee in this way and lose them for less than you should get, and, on the other hand, if you put too high a value on them, you will diminish the balance on which you will rank for dividend.

If you should find during the course of the sequestration that your security has fallen in value, you are entitled to amend your claim so as to give you right to a larger ranking as regards the future. No revaluation by you, however, of your security can affect any dividend which has previously been paid.

The trustee's right to call for a transfer to him of your security subsists during the whole period of the sequestration, but, of course, if you have sold your security, he cannot then ask for its transfer to him. On the other hand, you cannot revalue your security after the trustee has called upon you for a transfer. In calling upon you for such a transfer, however, the trustee must do so within a reasonable time after each revaluation, and this, as you know, always more or less depends upon the circumstances as well as the nature of the security.

The securities which require to be valued and deducted in your affidavit and claim are, however, only the securities which have been pledged with you by the bankrupt, or rather, to be more accurate, the securities which would, but for your pledge, have formed part of the bankrupt's estate. Consequently, securities given to you by or belonging to third parties are not to be valued or deducted, nor are guarantees or cautionary obligations, although it may be that these alone are good enough to pay your debt in full.

Having completed your affidavit and claim in this way, it is then lodged with the trustee along with your vouchers or other documents of debt-paid cheques, bills, &c. In due course these will be examined by the trustee, when he has completed his investigation of the bankrupt's affairs, and he will either admit you to a ranking as claimed for by you or to some lesser extent, or, it may be, reject your claim altogether for some stated reason. If you are dissatisfied with the ranking which the trustee gives, you are entitled to apply to the Court to have it amended, if you think there is good ground for that.

It is at this point that the strength or weakness of your position will be put to the test, and I propose to deal now with several possible positions and sets of circumstances from which lessons may be learned from the practical point of view.

It is an elementary rule in bankruptcy that there can be no double ranking—that is, the same debt cannot be ranked for twice. For example, if you have an overdrawn account in name of the bankrupt, and an accommodation bill with a third party's signature on it by way of security, you cannot claim in the bankruptcy for the amount of the bill plus the amount of the overdraft, as that would be claiming twice over for the same thing. You can only claim for the overdraft or for the sum in the bill as you prefer.

If you hold a guarantee for your debt, you are not bound to deduct the amount of it from your claim, even although the guarantor is absolutely good for the money. In such a case you rank on the estate for the full amount of your debt, and in so far as the dividend you receive is insufficient to meet your debt in full, you recover the balance from the guarantor up to the limit of his guarantee. For example, if you have an overdraft of £1000 and a good guarantee against it for £500, you nevertheless rank on the customer's estate for your full debt of £1000, and if you draw a dividend of, say, 10s. per £, this will give you £500, which, with the £500 you then receive from the guarantor, will square your account. If you were to deduct from your claim on the customer's estate the £500 coming from the guarantor, you would only rank for the balance of £500, and a dividend of 10s. per £ on that would only give you £250, making £750 in all, and leave you with a loss of £250. But, of course, that is not the position.

Normally, a guarantor who pays a part of your debt is entitled to rank on the bankrupt's estate for the amount he has paid to you, and as there can be no double ranking for the same debt, you would legally only be entitled to rank for the balance still due to you, and in the case I have just mentioned, you would sustain a loss of £250.

To prevent such a possibility, however, every bank guarantee contains an express agreement that the guarantor will not be entitled to rank on the estate for any payment he may have to make to you unless and until you have otherwise been paid in full. In other words, the guarantor contracts out of and gives up the right which he would otherwise have to rank direct on the estate.

Take next the position of a third party who has pledged his assets to you in security of the bankrupt's debt, but without giving you any personal obligation to pay in cash. Your whole right in this case consists in your ability to realise the assets in question, and whether these produce much or little, you have no further claim on that third party.

That third party, however, is in the same legal position as the guarantor, and he normally has a right to make a claim direct against the bankrupt's estate for the value of the assets he has given to you and which, in the circumstances, he has now lost. If, therefore, you have followed the usual practice and have not deducted the value of these assets from your claim, the result will be that the trustee will have received a double claim for the same debt to the value of these assets, and either your claim or the third party's claim will be rejected. To obviate this and to exclude the third party's right to claim in a case of this kind, the thing to do is just what is done in the case of a guarantee, and make the third party, when signing his letter of pledge, contract out of and give up the legal right which he would otherwise have to rank direct on the estate. It will be of interest to you to look up the form of letter of pledge which you use in this connection, and see whether the third party does actually give up this right. If you find he does not, I suggest that your form of letter of pledge requires amendment in this respect.

Theoretically your securities should all be complete and in good order at all times, but it is well known that, from the practical point of view, this is seldom possible, as you frequently find yourselves in the position that you have to take from your customer just what he may be willing to give you and be content, for example, with an incomplete or it may be a defective security.

Whenever, therefore, you hear of your customer's bankruptcy, or indeed learn of his public insolvency or impending bankruptcy, you should at once take stock of your position and get your securities over the bankrupt's assets completed and stamped up for the full amount, if that has not already been done, because you may be certain that the trustee will take all possible legal objection to your right to hold them. This does not apply to securities given to you by third parties, as the trustee has no interest in these, and you can deal with these at your convenience.

The first thing is to look at the stamp duty on

such of your security documents as have already been completed by registration or intimation. Sec. 88 (2) of the Stamp Act of 1891, as regards mortgage stamp duty in respect of future or fluctuating advances, provides as follows :—

> " Where such total amount is unlimited, the security is to be available for such an amount only as the *ad valorem* duty impressed thereon extends to cover, but where any advance or loan is made in excess of the amount covered by that duty the security shall, for the purpose of stamp duty, be deemed to be a new and separate instrument, bearing date on the day on which the advance or loan is made."

Accordingly where your security document bears *ex facie* to be in security of all sums due and to become due by your customer without any limit being stated, as is the case now in all modern forms, you require to consider whether sufficient mortgage stamp duty at 2s. 6d. per cent has been paid to cover the total amount of your advances. If not, the additional stamp duty should be paid without delay.

At the first glance that section of the Stamp Act would appear to limit your security to the amount which your deed is stamped to cover, and that, if any further duty is impressed on the deed within the sixty days preceding the bankruptcy, any additional security thereby obtained would be cut down under the 1696 Act. That, however, is not so. You will recollect that the 1696 Act relates only to voluntary acts on the part of the bankrupt, and the payment by you of additional stamp duty does not come under that category. Indeed, it is not an act of the bankrupt at all, so you are quite safe so far as regards additional stamping within the sixty days.

There is a further question, however, and that is : can you effectively add more stamp duty to your security document after your customer's bankruptcy has taken place ? The sound opinion seems to be that you can, although I cannot quote any precedent for the view. As you will see shortly, you can, in a race with the trustee in certain circumstances, even complete your title to the security after the bankruptcy, and, if that can be done, surely there is nothing to prevent you settling a debt which you owe to the Inland Revenue for the extra stamp duty and, if need be, the usual penalty for not stamping within the usual thirty days from the date of the additional advance. So far as you are concerned, however, you should endeavour to avoid the necessity for stamping your documents after the bankruptcy has commenced.

At the same time the case of *ex parte Wheeler* v. *The Trustee in Bankruptcy* (*in re* Warren) (1938, Ch. 725) must be remembered. In this case Warren, who was engaged in the building of houses on a building estate, was financed by Wheeler under an Agreement that Wheeler should guarantee Warren's overdraft, and in return any moneys paid to Warren's solicitors by advances from building societies or from sales, less the cost of site and expenses, should be lodged to the credit of Wheeler's account and was to be applied by him in reduction of Warren's overdraft and consequent relief of his own guarantee. A sum of £963, 9s. 3d. was thus lodged to the credit of Wheeler's account on the same day as, but at an earlier hour than, a receiving order in bankruptcy was made against Warren. Neither Wheeler nor the solicitors knew of any bankruptcy proceedings. It was held that the solicitors could not have acted with the moneys otherwise than in accordance with the arrangement, which created an equitable assignment in favour of the guarantor and was valid against the trustee.

In the previous lecture I explained to you how under the 1696 Act if, within sixty days of bankruptcy, a debtor voluntarily gave you a security for a past due debt, that security would be struck at. A past due debt in this sense does not necessarily mean one contracted prior to the commencement of the sixty days. The debt may be one contracted within the sixty days and no security or definite obligation for a security stipulated for at the time. If a security for such a debt incurred within the sixty days is thereafter voluntarily given by the debtor, it will be struck at.

Where, however, the security which you hold was not granted for a past due debt but for a new advance made at the time or for future advances, you are quite entitled to complete it by registration or intimation, as the case may be, within the sixty days preceding notour bankruptcy. This only applies, however, if you are in a position to complete your security without reference to the bankrupt. If you have to get any assistance from him, however slight, for example a signature or delivery of goods, or the key of a warehouse or it may be even a share certificate, then, if such assistance is a voluntary act on his part and not rendered under a previous definite legal obligation, your security will be ineffectual.

If you happen to hold as a security a delivery order in respect of goods belonging to the bankrupt in the custody of a neutral warehouse-keeper, then, notwithstanding the fact that you have already intimated your delivery order to the warehouse-keeper, or otherwise completed your title in his books, it is essential for you to make sure that your security is really effectual.

Such a security is only effectual if the goods represented by your delivery order have been identified and separated from other similar goods belonging to the debtor in the same warehouse. If, for example, your customer has 1000 sacks of flour stored in a warehouse and, by way of a security for your advances, gives you a delivery order for 100 of these, you must see that your 100 sacks are identified and separated from the other 900, so that, when you ask delivery of your lot, there will be no trouble with the trustee in ascertaining what is your lot. If that is not done the trustee will simply claim the whole.

If you find on reviewing your position while your customer's bankruptcy is impending—that is, prior to the date of the first deliverance—that the title to any of your securities is incomplete, you should proceed to have it completed without delay by having it registered or intimated or by doing whatever is required. If you get this done, you will be safe and beyond question, except where the security was taken for a past due debt.

If, however, the bankruptcy has commenced before you awoke to the fact, your position is different and you are now at a disadvantage as regards completing any incomplete securities which you may hold.

Under sec. 97 of the Bankruptcy Act the trustee's act and warrant, irrespective of its date, draws back to the date of the commencement of the bankruptcy—that is, the date of the first deliverance, and has the effect in law, as regards moveables, of actual delivery or an intimated assignation as the case may be, and, as regards heritage, of a decree of adjudication.

That appears to be wide in its sweep, and indeed is so but for two exceptions in which you may be interested and which are based on technicalities. The first relates to any unregistered share transfers which you may happen to hold, and these you may effectively produce to the companies for registration after the date of the bankruptcy, provided that the trustee has not produced his act and warrant to these companies before you present your transfers. The reason for this apparent exception from the sweep of the Act is that shares in a limited company can only be transferred by a formal transfer presented to the company and passed by the directors and the transferee accepted as a member of the company. No intimation of a transfer having been granted is of any use—the transfer itself must be presented and registered. So while the Act says that the trustee's act and warrant has the effect of an intimated assignation, that is saying nothing more than that it is of no effect in the case of shares in a limited company until it has been actually produced to the company as a transfer. Similar observations apply in the case of heritable property where, as you know, infeftment requires to be taken by means of the document being recorded in the register of sasines. You may, therefore, record your cash credit bond or *ex facie* absolute disposition, as the case may be, in the register of sasines after the commencement of the bankruptcy, provided that the trustee has not already recorded his act and warrant in that register.

In all other cases of incomplete security you are too late to take any steps at all for your protection after the date of the commencement of the bankruptcy. For example, unintimated assignations of life policies and interests in trust estates, unpresented delivery orders and so on, have all become valueless to you because, to be complete, they require intimation or delivery, as the case may be, while the trustee's act and warrant is itself intimation or delivery in these cases and is now prior in date to your intimation or delivery.

As regards incomplete securities your position, however, is rather different where the debtor's estate is being wound up under a trust deed. A trust deed, as I have said, is a private document and has no real legal effect unless and until the trustee has completed his title to the various assets belonging to the bankrupt by way of intimation, registration, infeftment and so on. In this way you are within your rights in completing title to all the securities which you may hold even after the granting of a trust deed, provided always that you do so before the trustee has completed his title. As we have seen in the case of a sequestration you cannot complete your title at all after the commencement of the bankruptcy to life policies, interests in trust estates and so on, but you can do so in the case of a trust deed, provided, of course, that you are first in the race with the trustee.

You will recollect what I said to you in the previous lecture with regard to specific appropriation and the rule as to general appropriation in the case of a current account as laid down in Clayton's case, and also the provisions of the 1696 Act which prevent you from taking from your debtor and completing within sixty days of his bankruptcy a security for a past due debt, and I want now to show you the practical application of these rules of law.

In *Robertson's Trustee* v. *The Union Bank* (1917, S.C. 549) the bank held a promissory note for £180 which had fallen due and of which payment was required. The customer then handed to the bank an assignation of a debt of £200 due to him by the Burgh of Paisley, drew a cheque on his current account with the bank for £180 and with that cheque paid the prior debt due to the bank under the promissory note. The trustee contended that the bank's security over the debt due by the burgh was bad because it was granted voluntarily within the sixty days in security of a past due debt. But the Court held that the bank were entitled to retain their security, not for the past due debt under the promissory note which had been paid off, but for the new debt incurred to them by the subsequent cheque drawn on the account. No doubt in substance it was pretty much the same debt, but the Court in this case had regard to the form which the transaction had followed and decided in favour of the bank.

One case I myself had will, I think, be sufficient to illustrate to you the application of these various rules from the practical point of view.

In the case I refer to, a bank had completed a security by way of an *ex facie* absolute disposition of the debtor's heritable property. This was taken for a past due debt at a time when the debtor was in very straitened financial circumstances and, as it turned out, within sixty days of his bankruptcy, which followed shortly afterwards.

After the security had been taken the same account was continued in the customer's name in the ledger without any break in its sequence. Various lodgments were then made to the credit of the account and, on the other hand, various withdrawals were made, but the debit balance continued to be maintained at practically the same level all the time.

The trustee in his investigation of the bankrupt's affairs discovered, of course, that this security had been granted within sixty days of the bankruptcy in respect of a debt which was then past due. He accordingly challenged the validity of the security under the 1696 Act and asked that the property be re-conveyed to him.

It was then pointed out to the trustee that, while it was true that the security in question had been granted for a past due debt and within sixty days of the bankruptcy and was therefore invalid so far as that past due debt was concerned, the bank nevertheless, following Robertson's case, claimed a right to hold the property for the new advances which they had made to the debtor after they had taken the security. It was maintained that these further advances were of the nature of *nova debita* and therefore fell within one of the three exceptions to the 1696 Act. The security was accordingly available to the bank for the amount of these new advances while the lodgments made after the security was taken went, in accordance with the rule in Clayton's case, to reduce or extinguish the old past due debt.

The trustee expressed himself satisfied with the position on the ground that, notwithstanding that the amount of the debt at the date of the bankruptcy was practically the same as the amount which had been due at the date when the security was taken, it was now a new debt incurred after the date of the security and for which the security was accordingly valid and effectual.

However, on thinking things over and looking into matters further, the trustee came forward again and challenged the security on the same grounds as before, but this time he pleaded specific appropriation of the new lodgments as against the new withdrawals, that is, of all the entries subsequent to the date of the security, the result of which was, he said, that the old past due debt remained as it was and that the security for it was bad. He tried to make out that the rule in Clayton's case did not apply because it was excluded by another method of appropriation which had been agreed upon between the bank and the customer. What he said was this—It was necessary for the customer to issue cheques to various trade creditors to keep his business going, and, as the bank would not make any additional advances, it was therefore necessary that the customer should pay in money to the credit of the account to enable these further cheques to be met. He produced copies of a number of letters from the customer to the bank agent showing or purporting to show that the various sums lodged to the credit of the account after the date of the security were specifically appropriated by being specially lodged for the purpose of meeting the new cheques which the debtor was now issuing to his trade creditors and could not be taken under Clayton's case as being in reduction of the old past due debt.

That would be a sound position for the trustee to take up if it could be established, and this is where you have to keep in mind the advice I previously gave you as to avoiding doing or saying or writing anything which might be construed as amounting to specific appropriation of any particular lodgments against any particular withdrawal.

As you know, when a customer has reached the limit of his advances with you he is usually told that he is not to issue any further cheques on his account without providing the necessary funds to meet them, or other similar expressions are used to the same effect. This is where danger lies for you, particularly where you wish the rule laid down in Clayton's case to apply so that your old debt may be paid off by the new lodgments and an entirely new debt created by the new withdrawals.

What you should do in all cases of this kind is to continue the account in an unbroken sequence and, if you can, get your customer to continue his operations on that account both by way of paying in and drawing out without, of course, increasing the amount of the debit balance. From what I have said you will appreciate that while your security may be bad as regards your past due debt on the one hand, it will be good as against the subsequent withdrawals on the other hand, and, to prevent this position being spoiled by any plea of specific appropriation, you must see that these subsequent withdrawals are not specially compensated or paid to you by specific appropriation of any of the new lodgments.

In such cases the instructions which you give to your customer should be that, in drawing any further cheques, he must see that the fixed limit of the advances is not exceeded, or other similar words to that effect. You should be careful not to say and particularly not to write to him saying that he is not to issue any further cheques unless he provides the necessary funds to meet them, or other similar words to that effect. It is this expression " to meet them " that does the damage. That is not what you want at all. What you want is that the new lodgments should be made to the general credit of the account, which will have the effect, in terms of Clayton's case, of reducing your old past due debt.

One question which frequently arises in banking practice is, as to whether and, if so, when the customer's existing account should be closed and a new one opened. The answer to that always depends upon whether it is in the bank's interest to do the one thing or the other.

In the case which I have just instanced of a security taken within what turns out to be the sixty days prior to the customer's bankruptcy, the proper thing undoubtedly to do is to continue to carry on the account in an unbroken sequence and to see that nothing in the nature of specific appropriation takes place. The same also applies where the bank may be making advances to a limited company to enable them to meet their wages, as in Freedman's case of which I told you in the previous lecture.

On the other hand, it is definitely in the interests of the bank to open a new account whenever the law draws a line across your account in one or other of the events which I previously mentioned to you where it is necessary that a personal obligation or a security for your debt should not be allowed to be extinguished by subsequent operations on the same account.

You will remember the case I quoted to you of *Christie & Ors.* v. *The Royal Bank*, where, through continuing the account without taking any notice of the death of a partner, the bank lost not only the personal obligation for the debt but also the security which they had. Also the cases of *Hopkinson* v. *Rolt, The Union Bank* v. *The National Bank*, and *Deeley* v. *Lloyds Bank*, where no attention was paid to intimations of postponed securities being granted, and the bank lost or seriously prejudiced their securities by continuing operations on the same account.

Here is a short summary of the principal occasions when your customer's overdrawn account should be closed and a new one opened so as to obviate a subsequent unpleasant position :—

1. Where your customer is a firm and a change in the partnership takes place by the death, retiral, assumption or bankruptcy of one of the partners.
2. Where you hold a security of any kind whether from your customer or from a third party, and you receive notice that a postponed or second mortgage has been granted over the same security subjects.
3. Where you hold a security of any kind and receive an arrestment which purports to attach assets in your hands belonging either to your customer or to a third party pledgor.
4. Where you have an either or survivor account and a security has been given to you by one of the parties and that party has now died.
5. Where your guarantor or one of several guarantors has died or become bankrupt.
6. Where your third party pledgor or one of several third party pledgors has died or become bankrupt.
7. Where your guarantor or third party pledgor or any one of several such intimates to you that you are no longer to make advances on the strength of his guarantee or pledge, as the case may be.

If you open a new account in any of these cases, the lodgments and withdrawals on that new account will be specifically appropriated thereto by the pay-in-slips and cheques being specially ear-marked—the account being styled, say, " No. 2 Account." In this way, these subsequent transactions are prevented from interfering with or disturbing the previous account on which you have stopped operations, thus ensuring the preservation of the personal obligations and securities which you hold therefor.

In closing an account and opening a new one in any of these cases, you will, of course, be careful to see that the old account is left open with its balance remaining at its debit. You will not under any circumstances transfer the debit balance from the old account to the new account, as otherwise you would completely spoil your position.

The seven occasions above mentioned where you should open a new account relate only to cases where your customer's account is overdrawn. If it should happen that the account is at credit at the time any one of these events happens, you can continue the same account and allow your customer to draw off the sum he has at his credit, but you cannot allow him any new advances on the strength of the guarantees or securities you hold until you have made a new arrangement with all the parties concerned.

LECTURE III.

ONCE you have got all your disputes and differences settled with the trustee and your claim admitted to a ranking, the question arises as to what is to be done with the securities you hold from the bankrupt, assuming that the trustee has not thought fit to take them over. In this connection you must remember that they are only securities and nothing more. You have no right of property in them—they do not belong to you absolutely.

Normally speaking, your stock exchange securities will be sold, life policies surrendered, deposit receipts uplifted and so on, and the proceeds of these will usually be just about the value you placed upon them in your affidavit and claim.

But there may be other items of security which are practically unrealisable at the moment and consequently of little or no value. These you may only be able to dispose of by practically giving them away, but, so long as there is no liability attaching to your holding them, the prudent course may appear to be to defer realising them meantime and nurse them in the hope of better times.

A good example in this connection is a life policy the surrender value of which may be very little. If you hold on to it and perhaps pay a premium or two—who knows what may happen ?

Now it may be through some stroke of luck—and it has happened before—that some unrealisable and valueless security, in the course of time, becomes valuable and is realised at a handsome increase. If that occurs, then, as that asset had never actually become your absolute property, but remained only a security from the beginning, you may require to do a little accounting. Assume, for example, that the realised proceeds of this particular security, when added to your other realisations of the bankrupt's assets in your hands and the dividends received from the estate, amount in all to more than your debt and interest, then you have been overpaid and the excess falls accordingly to be paid back by you to someone.

Usually that excess will fall to be paid over to the trustee, and, if the sequestration is closed and he has been discharged by that time, it may be that the creditors will have the sequestration opened up and the trustee reappointed or a new trustee appointed who will collect the excess from you and distribute it among the creditors in the shape of another dividend.

There is, however, such a thing in law as the abandonment of an asset by the trustee, and it may be, in such a case as I have figured, that the trustee has abandoned the asset in question and all his contingent rights in it. In such event, that abandonment enures to the bankrupt and not necessarily to you, and if the sequestration is closed and the trustee discharged, and if the bankrupt can make out a right on the ground of abandonment, then your accounting will be with him.

It may happen, however, that your debt was partly made up to you by a guarantor or by a third party pledgor, and if that was the case, then the excess in your hands will require to be accounted for to him so as to reimburse him in full before the trustee or the bankrupt can have any claim.

This position as regards a realised excess in the hands of a secured creditor arises from the fact that in Scotland we do not have any process of foreclosure whereby a right of security can be converted into a right of property. There is only one instance where that can be done here, and that is in connection with a security over heritable property under the Heritable Securities (Scotland) Act, 1894. A bondholder, and this includes a bank with a cash credit bond and disposition in security, who, having failed to obtain payment of his loan and having failed also to find a purchaser for the property by public auction, may apply to the Court for a foreclosure decree, whereupon the security subjects become his absolute property, and, when that has been granted, he is no longer bound to hold count and reckoning with the debtor for any excess or profit realised afterwards.

Where, however, the debt secured over a heritable property takes, as it often does in the case of a bank, the form of an *ex facie* absolute disposition qualified by the usual back letter, the law provides no remedy. The bank must continue to hold the property as a security right only until it has actually been sold or until a definite arrangement has been made with the trustee whereby he gives up to the bank his reversionary right in the property or, as it is sometimes called, the equity of redemption.

You will find this position discussed in the case of *The Clydesdale Bank Ltd.* v. *M'Intyre* (1909, S.C. 1405). In that case the bank had taken a security over a spinning mill by way of an *ex facie* absolute disposition qualified by a back letter. A feu-duty of £152 per annum was payable in respect of the security subjects, and as the income from the property was insufficient to meet the outgoings, the bank were desirous of having the security subjects taken back by their debtor and so avoiding further liability for the feu-duty, owner's rates, &c. The debtor, however, declined to take back the property with its onerous burdens, so the bank raised an action to compel him to do so. In this action, the Court granted decree in favour of the bank, and the debtor accordingly accepted and recorded a reconveyance of the property in his favour as a result of which the bank were relieved of the liabilities of ownership, and particularly of the liability for the heavy feu-duty which they had incurred under their *ex facie* absolute disposition.

While that case ended satisfactorily for the bank, I should warn you, if you ever find yourselves in a similar position, that you should not follow the same course and take action against the debtor to compel him to take the security subjects back. If he will not readily agree to do this, you should seek some other remedy, such as a sale of the property for what it will fetch.

The reason for this warning is that while you may be successful in obtaining a decree of the Court ordaining the debtor to take his property back and record a reconveyance of it, there is no law which can compel the debtor to do so. All he has to do is to insist in his refusal notwithstanding the decree of the Court, and, if he does that, you are helpless. It is true he may be punished for contempt of Court in refusing to obey such an *ad factum præstandum* decree, but that does not get your name off the register of sasines or that of the debtor inserted therein instead, and until that has been done your liabilities as owner of the property still continue.

There are circumstances where the Court, having granted an *ad factum præstandum* decree, will authorise some third party to carry it out in the event of the defender refusing or failing to do so, but the recording of a reconveyance in the register of sasines cannot be done by anyone except the defender himself or his authorised law agent on his behalf.

Sec. 141 of the titles to Land Consolidation (Scotland) Act, 1868, deals with this subject, and enacts that all deeds presented for registration in the register of sasines must have a warrant of registration written thereon on behalf of the grantee, and this warrant must be signed by such grantee or by his authorised law agent. No other signature will do whether appointed by the Court or not. The keeper of the register will not accept anything but the signature of the grantee or his authorised law agent as provided for in the Act.

We now come to deal with the last phase of a bankruptcy, that is, the recovery of your customer's unpaid balance from his guarantor or third party pledgor with the view of having the account in your ledger squared off in one way or another.

Where there are several guarantors, whether under one joint and several guarantee or under several separate guarantees, they are, among themselves, ultimately liable only for their *pro rata* share of the debt. Accordingly a guarantor paying the whole debt or a share of the debt greater than his proportionate share forthwith becomes entitled to claim from each of his co-guarantors a rateable contribution so as to recoup him for the excess which he has paid beyond his own proper share. This apportionment of the loss is calculated according to the maximum amount for which each guarantor is legally liable in terms of his guarantee.

Third party pledgors are in law just guarantors, and they accordingly have the same rights of relief, contribution, and recovery *inter se*. The only difference between them is that the guarantor has still to put his hand in his pocket and pay you in cash, while the third party pledgor has already yielded up to you the maximum of his liability.

It is always open to you to call upon any one of your guarantors or to realise any one of your third party pledges if by doing so you will have sufficient to provide the balance of the debt. If you care, you can deal with them one after the other. You do not require to call upon all your guarantors at the same time or to realise all your third party pledges at the same time. Further, you are not interested in seeing that each guarantor or third party pledgor bears his own proper share of the loss—that is a matter for them to arrange among themselves. If, as sometimes happens, one of your guarantors, who has been called upon to pay the whole of the debt, offers to pay up only his *pro rata* share of the loss and suggests that you recover the balance from his co-guarantors, you should not agree. You may, however, take a payment from him expressly to account of his liability, but you must not give him a full discharge except on payment of his maximum liability, otherwise you will spoil your position with the other guarantors, who will be entitled to demand a similar benefit, if not to escape liability altogether.

The amount to be paid by your guarantor will

be the whole debt due by your bankrupt customer, but not exceeding the limited principal sum specified in the guarantee with such an amount of interest as you may be entitled to under the wording of the guarantee. Practically speaking, no two guarantees are in exactly the same terms. Each bank seem to prefer their own form, presumably because they think it is better than the form used by any other bank. Consequently, the amount of interest payable by a guarantor may be more in one case and less in another.

For example, the interest due by a guarantor under one form of document may be limited to interest on the principal sum guaranteed and no more, while, under another form, he may be responsible for the whole interest on the account without any limit. Whatever may be the guarantor's liability, whether only for interest on the principal sum guaranteed or for interest on the whole of the customer's debt, the period over which you can calculate that interest depends not only on the state of the account but also upon the particular terms of the guarantee.

The position as regards this matter is that the guarantor is entitled to expect that you will conduct the customer's overdrawn account with you in strict accordance with the usual practice and follow the usual methods of accounting, and that you will not make any departure from that course to his prejudice without his consent.

It is the normal practice of banks to apply the interest to the account each half year—that is, place the amount of the interest due down to date to the debit of the account. Now, even although your customer pays you nothing at all thereafter, you cannot say that that interest which you have applied to the account is still due to you as interest. It is certainly still due to you, but only as capital and not as interest. The reason for this is that the law regards the amount which you have debited to the account in name of interest as being nothing but a further advance of capital to your customer to enable him to pay the interest, and that interest is accordingly deemed to have been paid to you.

As regards a third party pledge this very seldom contains any limitation of the pledgor's liability, which therefore is just exactly what the pledge will realise at any given date and no more. There is no objection, however, to such a document containing a limitation to a specified sum and interest, in which case the same considerations apply as in the case of a guarantee.

In cases where your guarantees and pledges are not sufficient to meet the whole of your debit balance, then assuming you have recovered everything you can, there is nothing left to be done except to carry your recoveries to the credit of the account and the unpaid balance to profit and loss and finally close off the account.

In cases where your guarantees and pledges, however, are sufficient or, it may be, more than sufficient to meet the whole of your debit balance, there are two possible positions among the guarantors and pledgors. The first is where each one has contributed to the full extent of his liability. In such a case if you have an excess in hand, that excess will fall to be paid back by you to them *pro rata* and in proportion to the sums contributed. The other position is where each has not contributed to the full extent of his liability—that is, one may have contributed his whole share and another may have contributed only a part of his share. An adjustment among them in such a

182

case becomes essential so as to put them all on the same *pro rata* basis, but that is not a matter with which you should readily deal. It is always far better to allow the parties themselves to adjust and settle their various claims *inter se* and then make a joint request to you to pay over the excess in your hands to them in certain specified proportions so as to put them all on the same footing. If you do happen to have an excess in your hands in a case where the parties cannot agree, you can, if you wish to be rid of the whole thing, raise an action of multiplepoinding and pay the excess into Court, where the parties can fight out the question for themselves.

So far, we have been dealing with cases where the settlements with the guarantors and third party pledgors take place after the bankruptcy, but it sometimes happens that it is necessary for you to deal with the matter before the bankruptcy takes place and this is where complications and difficulties arise. The practice in such circumstances is not the same in all banks.

Suppose your guarantor intimates to you that you are not to make any further advances to your customer on the strength of his guarantee, you will, of course, stop operations on the account and open a new account to which all subsequent transactions will be specifically appropriated as previously explained. You may then call upon your guarantor to settle his liability under his guarantee or, without the necessity for your doing that, he may come to you and offer to settle. His liability as regards principal is in such circumstances the amount at the debit of the old account —say £500 (assuming that his guarantee is for a greater sum), less the credit balance, if any, on the new account—say £100. He is entitled to the benefit of that credit balance, because the total indebtedness of your customer on all his accounts is now only £400. What he is not entitled to is the benefit of the lodgments to the credit of the new account—only the credit balance.

Up to this point the matter is easy, but what you do next requires thought on your part as well as on the part of the guarantor. Usually the guarantor is so glad to be relieved of his liability and the bank agent so glad to get the money that they omit to ask one another—what is this that we do ?

In order to concentrate your minds on this problem, we can once more take Whatmough's case as a basis to work on. You will remember that Whatmough owed the British Linen Bank a sum of roughly £7300, which had stood at the debit of his dormant account for a matter of three months before he paid it off, and that, during that period, he was, to say the least of it, in a very doubtful financial position. Now suppose that the bank had held a guarantee for £1000 from A. against Whatmough's debt and another separate guarantee from B. also for £1000. And suppose further that during that period of three months guarantor A. came to the conclusion that, for some reason or another, he would be better to pay his £1000 to the bank and get rid of his liability altogether.

At this stage I think I cannot do better than quote to you a paragraph from Wallace & M'Neil, p. 300, dealing with such a situation. It is as follows :—

> When a guarantor pays the amount of his guarantee before the sequestration of the principal debtor and receives delivery of his

guarantee although with a receipt endorsed thereon containing a reservation in the following or like terms—

This payment is accepted under reservation of and without prejudice to our right to claim on the estate of the said X.Y. for the full amount of his indebtedness,

and where the amount so received is placed to the credit of a separate account in the books of the bank in the name of the agent for the obligations of the guarantor, on the subsequent sequestration of the principal debtor the bank are bound to deduct from the amount of their claim the payment so received from the guarantor. It has been decided in *Mackinnon's Trustee* v. *The Bank of Scotland* (1915, S.C. 411) that payments from a guarantor prior to sequestration must be deducted (*i.e.*, in the bank's affidavit and claim) whatever may have been the terms of the guarantee under which the payments were made. It is respectfully thought this decision requires reconsideration.

and with that opinion I entirely agree.

However, as that is the law—for the time being at least—it must be followed, and accordingly what the British Linen Bank agent would have done in the case supposed, would be to take the £1000 from guarantor A., give him back his guarantee with any desired form of receipt thereon, and place the amount to the credit of Whatmough's account.

When that is done the guarantee would appear to be at an end, and guarantor A., instead of being a guarantor any longer, would now become the direct creditor of Whatmough for the £1000 with right to rank direct in the subsequent sequestration. No doubt he would think that was a clever thing to do, because he himself would now receive the dividend on his £1000 instead of allowing the bank to rank for it and keep it. But would that have been a clever thing ? Just remember what happened. Whatmough, as you know, made a special effort and paid off his overdraft in full, and accordingly guarantor B. would not be called upon by the bank to pay anything at all. In these circumstances guarantor A. would have prejudiced his position very seriously. He had elected to change his legal status from that of a guarantor to that of an ordinary creditor of Whatmough. The dividend he would get on his claim in the subsequent sequestration would be a mere trifle, but, as against that, he had lost all claim for relief against guarantor B., who had an absolute answer to any such claim, and he had also lost all claim against the bank in the event of their later on having an excess of recoveries.

In circumstances such as these what would be the proper arrangement for a guarantor to make with the bank when he wished to relieve himself and his estate of further liability and at the same time protect and preserve his rights of relief against the bank in the event of there being excess recoveries and against his co-guarantors for their *pro rata* share of the loss ? There is only one course I know of which will achieve that purpose, and that is for the guarantor to hand over to the bank the sum specified in the guarantee to be held by the bank, not in settlement or discharge of his liability, but merely as a security for the due implement of his guarantee. A simple acknow- ledgment and nothing more would then be given

186

by the bank for the money, which would be placed to the credit of a special account or on deposit receipt in name of the bank's agent or other official. The guarantee would remain in the hands of the bank and the customer's account would be unaffected. The relationship of guarantor and banker and all that it implies would be continued undisturbed. Then, if the customer paid off his overdraft, as Whatmough did, or even reduced it, or if there should later be excess recoveries in the hands of the bank, or if there should be rights of relief against another guarantor or third party pledgor, the guarantor who had provided for his liability in advance in this way would be in a sound position and all that he would pay for that would be the mere cost of giving up to the bank the right to draw a dividend in the subsequent sequestration of the customer's estate, which might turn out to be next to nothing.

You will notice that some banks stipulate in their form of guarantee that they are to be entitled to retain the guarantee even on payment by the guarantor of his full liability. Presumably this is done to enable the bank to rank on the customer's estate for the full amount of the debt notwithstanding the terms of the decision in *Mackinnon's Trustee* v. *The Bank of Scotland*. Such a clause does not seem to be effectual for that purpose, and in any case it does not make it clear whether the relationship of the guarantor to the bank or to the other guarantors and third party pledgors still exists or has been cancelled.

I mentioned to you that where your guarantor intimated prior to your customer's bankruptcy that you were not to make any further advances to your customer on the strength of his guarantee and later came to settle up with you, the sum due by him was the amount at the debit of the old account minus the balance, if any, at the credit of the new account.

A different position arises, however, where the first step is taken prior to your customer's bankruptcy by you and not by the guarantor. Suppose that, prior to the bankruptcy, you decide to call upon the guarantor to pay up under his guarantee. I want you to think what this involves. Some guarantees contain a clause to the effect that the bank are to be entitled to call upon a guarantor for a payment or payments to account of his liability. If you do decide to call upon your guarantor for payment prior to the customer's bankruptcy, what course would you propose to follow ? Would you continue to allow your customer to go on paying in and drawing out, and, if so, would you continue these operations on the same account or would you open a new one ? When calculating the amount due by the guarantor, would you say it was the amount at the debit of the old account minus the whole lodgments to the credit of the new account or minus only the credit balance on that account ? What would you do with the money so paid by the guarantor ? What kind of receipt would you give him ? Would you hand him back his guarantee ? There is little or no law on this aspect of the position, that is, where it is you and not the guarantor who makes the first move prior to your customer's bankruptcy, and anything I might say would be a mere matter of opinion. My advice to you in such a case where you feel that you really must do something with your guarantor at once, is either (1) call upon your guarantor to give you security for the due fulfilment of his guarantee, in which case everybody's legal position is preserved—don't call upon the guarantor to make a payment to account or to settle his liability or indebtedness under the guarantee ; in that case nobody will know where he is ; or (2) call up your overdraft and stop all dealings with your customer ; you can then go ahead with your call on the guarantor without becoming involved in an impossible position.

On every one of the various occasions which I have mentioned to you, where you should close an old account and open a new one, subsequent transactions being specifically appropriated to the new account, a point has been raised as to the legal effect of such specific appropriation in a question, not with your guarantor or third party pledgor, but with your customer's trustee in bankruptcy.

Assume that you have closed an old account with a debit balance for the purpose of preserving your rights against a deceased partner, or guarantor or third party pledgor, and have opened a new account in name of your customer for the subsequent transactions, and that there is a credit balance on the new account. In the event of your customer's bankruptcy in that position of matters you wish, of course, to be able to say to the representatives of the deceased partner or guarantor or third party pledgor that they have no interest in the lodgments to the credit of the new account, and at the same time you wish to say to the trustee on your customer's bankrupt estate that he has no interest in the sum at the credit of the new account until the debit on the old account has been paid.

In such circumstances it has been contended for the trustee on your customer's bankrupt estate that the arrangement was that the lodgments to the credit of the new account were specifically appropriated to meet the withdrawals on that same account and nothing else, and that, therefore, you could not hold the credit balance on the new account against any other debt due to you by the bankrupt.

There are several cases with regard to the effect of specific appropriation in a case of this kind, but, unfortunately, they are not all in agreement. You may, however, proceed in such a case on the basis that in a question with the trustee on your customer's bankrupt estate you are not bound to pay over to him the balance at the credit of the new account without deducting the debit balance due on the old account. The reason for this is that the arrangement for specific appropriation adopted in the circumstances in question was only so adopted in a question with and to fix and preserve the liability of the representatives of the deceased partner, guarantor or third party pledgor as regards the old account, and to prevent their obtaining the benefit of the lodgments to the credit of the new account as they would otherwise have had under the rule laid down in Clayton's case.

Before closing, I would like to deal with a very interesting position which you should constantly keep before you in connection with your securities not only over heritable property but also over stock exchange and other classes of security.

The following observations may not appear to you to be very closely related to the subject of these lectures — " Bankruptcy and its Consequences "—but they are of the utmost importance to you. Every debtor in your books should be regarded by you as a potential bankrupt and your transactions with him should be regulated accordingly. When a bankruptcy takes place one of the first things the trustee does is to scrutinise the bankrupt's financial position and the various transactions he has had with you and others with the view of searching out all possible sources from which money may be drawn for the general body of creditors, or it may even be to meet his own fee, and you can take it that if the trustee finds any weakness in your position on an application of the principles of specific appropriation or extinction of securities you will hear about it. With the view, therefore, of keeping you out of troubles if and when your customer's bankruptcy does come along, I have thought it well to emphasise fully the practical application of the lessons to be drawn by you from Clayton, *Christie* v. *The Royal Bank, The Union Bank* v. *The National Bank,* and so on.

The rule laid down in the various cases I mentioned is this—when you hold a security over any property for past and future advances and receive intimation that your customer has granted a postponed security over the same property to a third party, as he is always perfectly entitled to do, any further advances which you may make to your customer thereafter cannot rank on the property or security subjects in priority to the postponed charge. Such further advances would, however, be secured after the postponed creditor had received payment of his debt in full, that is, assuming that the property was of sufficient value to pay all the debts.

Whenever, therefore, you receive intimation of a postponed security having been granted by your customer over property of any kind already pledged to you, it is, as I mentioned before,

essential for your protection that you stop operations on the account and, if need be, open a new
account which will always be at credit or, if not,
the balance on which you will know ranks on the
security subjects only after the third party's debt
has been paid.

If you do not do this, and continue instead to
allow the operations to continue on the original
account, the balance due to you at the date of the
intimation is all that you have a security for,
and by the subsequent operations, and particularly
the lodgments to the credit of the account, that
balance will be wiped out and a new debit balance
created in respect of which you will have no
security or at the most only a postponed security,
which may be valueless.

Rights in third parties may emerge in security
subjects held by you otherwise than by formal
intimation of a postponed bond or assignment.
For example, an arrestment lodged in your hands
by a creditor of your customer attaches all sums
in your hands belonging to him. Even although
there may be a debit balance on your customer's
current account the arrestment will attach his
reversionary right in the securities which he had
pledged with you, and consequently your rights
against the subjects of the pledge will, as regards
any further advances which you may make, be
postponed to the arrestment. And if you allow
operations to continue on the account you may
lose your security altogether.

In the cases which I have quoted to you, the
granting of the postponed security was always
formally intimated to the bank who held the first
security, but I am unable to tell you whether it
is necessary that formal intimation be given or
whether something less will do. You might, for

example, be informed by your customer verbally that he had granted such a postponed security, or it might be by the postponed security holder himself telling you, or you may have received reliable information on the subject from some other source.

From the point of view of the postponed security holder, it is desirable that he should give formal intimation and be able to prove that he did so, but supposing that were not done and the postponed security holder later on undertook to prove, and did prove, that although you did not get formal intimation, you were well aware of what had been done and what his position in the matter was. It seems to me in that case that, having at least knowledge of the existence of the second charge on the property, you would not be acting in good faith if you made any further advances to your customer and endeavoured to rank these prior to the security held by the postponed creditor. That would be a very weak position to be in, and consequently my advice to you is that in all cases whenever you have knowledge of the existence of a postponed charge affecting your security subjects, whether given to you formally or informally, and whether given by the postponed creditor or your customer or any other person, you should at once take steps to stop further operations on the account until matters have otherwise been adjusted to your satisfaction.

In this connection I think I should inform you of my own experience as to a method by which a bank may be charged with knowledge of the existence of a postponed security.

In my own office, we hold on behalf of banks a number of titles of various heritable properties over which they have securities. The proprietors of these properties or their solicitors sometimes ask for a loan of the titles on the usual borrowing receipt, and sometimes explain the reason for their request and sometimes not. Quite frequently the titles may be required by them to enable them to look into some question which has perhaps arisen with a neighbouring proprietor as to whether a boundary wall is mutual or not, or as to the details of a servitude, right of access, drainage, and so on.

When these titles are returned after the purpose has been served, I generally examine the search just to see what the proprietor of these particular security subjects has been doing, and from it I have found on several occasions that he has borrowed further money from some third party to whom he has granted a postponed bond which now appears in the search and for the first time comes to light.

At first I was in a dilemma as to what, if anything, I should do in such a case, as obviously no formal intimation of the granting of the postponed security had been given to the bank, and the bank had no knowledge direct or indirect as to that having been done. Ultimately I came to the conclusion that as I had information as to the existence of the postponed security, and as I was the agent of the bank, and as the knowledge of an agent is held to be the knowledge of his principal, my duty was to communicate the information to the bank and afford them the opportunity of stopping operations on the account or taking such other steps as they might think necessary.

In some cases, however, the search does not form one of the documents of title delivered to the bank in connection with the security, and in these circumstances it is not possible to obtain information on a point of this kind.

So long as you do not have actual knowledge of the existence of a postponed security you are perfectly safe with regard to your continuing advances. Registration of a postponed bond in the register of sasines, although appearing in the public records, is not of itself sufficient to put you in bad faith in making subsequent advances, but, on this point, I should not like to be dogmatic, as it is just possible that the Court, if the question ever arose, might take a different view.

The decision of 1886 in the case of *The Union Bank* v. *The National Bank* was based on the first security being constituted by way of an *ex facie* absolute disposition and relative back letter, and, as we saw, the Court decided that the advances made by the National Bank after receipt of intimation of the Union Bank's postponed security were not covered. There is a question here as to whether the principle underlying that decision would have been applicable had the first security held by the National Bank taken the form of a cash credit bond and disposition in security.

Owing to the technicalities of Scots conveyancing and the provisions of the 1696 Act it is not possible to take a security over heritable property for an indefinite sum or for a sum to be advanced in the future. An ordinary bond and disposition in security in statutory form will not achieve that object, and it is therefore necessary to proceed not by way of a deed which bears *ex facie* to be a security but by way of a document which on the face of it conveys the property itself to the creditor. Hence the use of *ex facie* absolute dispositions coupled with unrecorded back letters.

One objection, however, to a creditor taking his security in the form of an *ex facie* absolute disposition is that immediately he puts his deed on the record he becomes personally responsible for all the obligations of ownership under the title. That is, he becomes personally liable to pay the feu-duty and to implement the building and other similar conditions contained in the titles and which may be very onerous.

Where the title conditions are such as to render a security by way of an *ex facie* absolute disposition undesirable from a creditor's point of view, the only alternative is to take a document which on the face of it bears to be in security only.

Where you are dealing with the case of a security for a fixed loan all of which is advanced at the beginning, the ordinary statutory form of a bond and disposition in security is appropriate, but it is not appropriate to cover the case of advances on a current account the amount of which fluctuates from day to day.

A suitable form of document to meet the case of a fluctuating security has accordingly been provided under the Judicial Procedure, &c. (Scotland), Act, 1856, which authorises a valid security for a fluctuating and future debt in the form of a cash credit bond and disposition in security provided that the maximum sum secured, which may include three years' interest at 5 per cent, is specifically set forth. That Act provides that securities taken in that form shall be equally valid and effectual as if the whole sums advanced upon the current account had been paid at or prior to the date of the deed or the date of its registration, and that such security should remain and subsist to the extent of the specified sum or any lesser sum until the current account is finally closed and the balance paid up.

Now, in view of the explicit terms of that Act

as to the security under a cash credit bond being available until final settlement for the full sum specified, the question arises as to whether the principle applied in the case of *The Union Bank* v. *The National Bank* applies at all, where the holder of a cash credit bond of this kind receives formal intimation of the granting of a postponed security by his debtor, and whether is he in safety thereafter to make further advances to the debtor ? In the Union Bank case where it was an *ex facie* absolute disposition, the prior creditor was held to have no right to make further advances after receiving intimation, but would the position have been just the same had it been a cash credit bond ? I have discussed this with several whose opinions are not to be disregarded, and they think that intimation of a second security cannot affect future advances under a prior cash credit bond. Having regard to the decision in *Deeley* v. *Lloyd's Bank Ltd.*, and particularly to Lord Shaw's opinion that there is no difference in this respect between the law of Scotland and the law of England, I cannot but take the view that a security by way of a cash credit bond is open to the same objection as a security under an *ex facie* absolute disposition when it comes to a postponed creditor giving intimation of his rights.

You will therefore appreciate that this principle, which apparently applies to one class of document as well as to another, applies equally to any one class of property as well as to any other, so that in all cases whenever you have knowledge, however obtained, of a third party acquiring an interest in your security subjects whether by postponed bond, assignment, arrestment or otherwise, you will be well advised to proceed with great caution and stop operations on the account until other arrangements are made with your customer for his future transactions. If you do this you will avoid the danger of having your secured debt wiped out under the rule of Clayton's case, and avoid having your further advances postponed to the second creditor's advances under the principle of the Union Bank case.

The general rule of law in Scotland with regard to the validity of any security is that it must be completed in the person of the creditor by actual or constructive delivery in the case of moveables and by registration or intimation in the case of other forms of property, but there are two specialties in this connection to which I should draw your attention.

In England the rules of law are not quite the same as with us, and one of the variations is to be found, for example, in what is known there as a floating charge granted by a limited company. Such a charge may be granted by a company in England by way of security for a fixed or a fluctuating debt, and, on being registered in terms of the Companies Acts, will constitute a valid security on the company's undertaking and assets according to the terms and conditions of the document.

Such a floating charge does not necessarily affect the various assets of the company so long as it is carrying on business in the usual way, but it comes into force on the company going into liquidation. In that event the liquidator winding up the business and affairs of the company gives effect to the charge in the distribution of the proceeds of realisation of the assets. A floating charge may also contain provisions for the creditor appointing a receiver in certain events to take charge of all or any of the assets which may be covered by it.

In Scotland such a floating charge is of no effect because it does not comply with our rule as to the necessity for delivery in the case of moveables or registration or intimation in the case of other forms of property. While, however, a limited company registered in Scotland cannot grant a floating charge over its assets in Scotland, it has been held that a company registered in England may grant such a security over its assets in Scotland, both heritable and moveable, without the creditor obtaining delivery and registering a bond or disposition or assignation or other deed as would normally be required here.

In this connection I would refer you to the case of *Anchor Line (Henderson Bros.) Ltd.* (1937, Ch. 483). That company was registered in England but carried on business in Scotland, where it owned considerable heritable and moveable assets. Some time before going into liquidation it granted a floating charge in favour of the Union Bank of Scotland Ltd. in security of all sums advanced and to be advanced by them. The charge was duly registered with the Registrar of Companies in England in terms of the Companies Acts, and was expressed to be a first charge, ranking after certain prior mortgages or bonds over the company's undertaking and all its property and assets whatsoever and wheresoever by way of a floating security, and no further mortgages or charges were to rank prior or *pari passu*.

In the winding up a question was raised as to how far, if at all, that floating charge was effectual as regards the company's heritable and moveable property in Scotland in view of the fact that the bank had not obtained delivery of the moveables and had no other completed security deed relating to the heritable and other assets.

The Court held that the liquidator who had realised all the various assets was bound to observe the rules of law operating in England, as the liquidation was that of a company registered there, and that he must give effect to the floating charge in accordance with its terms. This meant that the charge was, notwithstanding the rules of Scots law, effectual as a security over all the company's assets in Scotland, and gave to the bank a preference which they would not have had if the company had been registered in Scotland, unless they had taken the precaution of obtaining delivery of the moveable assets and had registered or intimated formal security writs relating to the other assets.

The other specialty I referred to relates to bills of lading and other similar documents of title to goods. Possession of these documents of title, as you know, is under the Factors Act, 1889, equivalent to the possession of the goods themselves and is accordingly sufficient to constitute a valid security over the goods.

In the case of such documents you can, under certain circumstances, part with the possession of them in such a way as not to lose your rights therein notwithstanding the rules of law I mentioned before, but, of course, you require to be careful in your actings in the matter.

You may, for example, hand over such documents of title to an agent on your behalf to enable him to receive delivery of the goods and dispose of them for you. In such a case he holds the documents and the goods as trustee on your behalf, and you do not lose your rights therein until they have been sold. You may, if you care, appoint your debtor, to whom the goods really belong, to be your agent and trustee in the matter, and, if you see that your trust letter setting forth the true position is in order, you will be quite safe in the event of your debtor's bankruptcy. It will not necessarily protect you, however, from fraud on his part.

Such a trust letter is usually granted by your debtor to you, and should acknowledge receipt of the documents and state that the granter undertakes to act as your agent and trustee in the sale of the goods and to remit the entire net proceeds to you. The letter should also bear that the transaction is to be kept separate from any other, and that the granter is to insure the goods and to return them or the balance remaining unsold to you on demand.

You do, however, run a risk in such a transaction as is illustrated in the case of *Lloyds Bank Ltd.* v. *The Bank of America, &c.* (1938, 2 K.B. 147). In that case a company had pledged bills of lading with Lloyds Bank, who thereupon handed them back to the company for the sole purpose of effecting a sale of the goods—the proceeds to be held in trust for that bank.

Instead of selling the goods as arranged, the company pledged the documents with the Bank of America in security of advances from them. That bank acted in good faith in the matter and had no knowledge that the company were under any obligation to Lloyds Bank to hold and sell for them.

The company while still indebted to both banks became insolvent, and, on learning what had happened, Lloyds Bank claimed the return of the documents or their value from the Bank of America.

In the subsequent action the Court held that while the company, in view of the terms of their arrangement with Lloyds Bank, had no title to deal with the documents or the goods except as trustee agents and that that bank were the true owners, nevertheless the company, being mercantile agents and in possession of the documents of title within the meaning of the Factors Act, 1889, were in a position to make a valid pledge of the documents to the Bank of America, who were, therefore, held to be entitled to retain the documents and the goods represented thereby.

Sec. 2 (1) of the Factors Act, 1889, provides :—

> " Where a mercantile agent is, with the consent of the owner, in possession of goods or of the documents of title to goods, any sale, pledge, or other disposition of the goods, made by him when acting in the ordinary course of business of a mercantile agent, shall, subject to the provisions of this Act, be as valid as if he were expressly authorised by the owner of the goods to make the same ; provided that the person taking under the disposition acts in good faith, and has not at the time of the disposition notice that the person making the disposition has not authority to make the same."

You will, therefore, see that, on handing back documents of title to your debtor on the usual trust letter for the purpose of effecting a sale of goods on your behalf, you will still remain the owner of the goods and be protected in the case of your debtor's bankruptcy, but you will always be exposed to the risk of fraudulent actings on his part.

Banking Transactions Reviewed
by the Courts

LECTURE I.

THE common law implies in the case of every citizen a general rule of careful conduct towards others and regard for their interests, and it makes provision in some form or other for penalising anyone who ignores that rule and causes loss or injury to another.

A banker is in no different position from any other person in that respect. He is, for example, liable at common law to his customer if, neglecting that rule, he pays a cheque which bears a false indorsement, even although he acted in perfectly good faith and without any suspicion of the existence of a forgery. In the same way a banker at common law is liable to a third party, that is, to the true owner, if he acts in the collection of a cheque on which there is a forged indorsement.

In view of the exigencies of a banker's business, however, certain limited measures of protection have been given to him by various statutes, but he is only entitled to claim that protection if he conforms to the conditions laid down by these statutes.

These statutory immunities are, of course, familiar to you. I need not do more than remind you that the first of these is sec. 19 of the Stamp Act of 1853, which protects a banker paying any draft or order drawn upon him and payable to order on demand which purports to be indorsed by the payee and that without reference to whether the banker acts in the ordinary course of business or without negligence, although, as a matter of fact, good faith will be expected in every case although not expressly mentioned.

Then there is sec. 60 of the Bills of Exchange Act of 1882 which protects a paying banker in similar circumstances where an open cheque is involved, provided in this case that the payment is made in good faith and in the ordinary course of business. Sec. 80 of that Act protects a paying banker in similar circumstances in the case of payment of a crossed cheque, provided that he obeys the statutory instruction contained in the crossing and acts in good faith and without negligence.

So far as the collecting banker is concerned, the only protection which he has is that under sec. 82 of the 1882 Act where he collects a crossed cheque. Then he is entitled to immunity, but only on condition that he acts in good faith and without negligence and that he collects the cheque for a customer.

You will observe that these sections, which refer to the banker acting in good faith and in the ordinary course of business or without negligence, do not impose on him any new or additional burdens or conditions to which he was not subject at common law. All these things and more are and have all along been expected of him at common law, and the real effect of these sections is rather to tone down the rigour of the common law for the benefit of the banker.

Notwithstanding the immunities conferred upon bankers by these sections, it is the case, unfortunately, that the conditions upon which these immunities have been granted have not been complied with in many instances, as is shown by the numerous reports of litigations in which bankers have been involved from 1882 onwards.

These litigations have involved not only paying bankers, but also collecting bankers, and have been founded upon complaints against them by their customers as well as by third parties. The grounds of these complaints, as set forth in the summonses against the bankers, are usually negligence and frequently conversion. Lawyers, in framing their summonses, endeavour to make them as comprehensive as they can and insert all possible grounds of complaint in the hope that if they should happen to fail on one ground they will succeed on another.

Most of these litigations have taken place in England, and you will notice that in a great many of them the grounds of complaint are stated as conversion or, alternatively, negligence or, alternatively, for money had and received on behalf of the plaintiff.

The expression money had and received on account of the plaintiff practically describes itself, but in Scotland we would refer to such an action as one for an accounting.

A person charged with conversion, which is purely an English term, has been described as anyone who, however innocently, obtains possession of the property of another, who has been fraudulently deprived of the possession of it, and disposes of it whether for his own benefit or that of another person.

There is no precisely corresponding term known to Scots Law, but from that description of what constitutes conversion we can visualise to some extent what is meant, although probably we would give it a somewhat harsher name.

The remaining ground of complaint—negligence —has been judicially described in these words:—

"Negligence is the doing of that which a reasonable man, under all the circumstances of the particular case in which he is acting, would not do, or the failure to do something which a reasonable man under those circumstances, would do."

That seems on the first reading to be a very fair definition of what constitutes negligence, but you must not be misled by the expression " a reasonable man." That expression means a reasonable man in the eyes of the law, which is an entirely different thing from the average man or the man in the street.

There have been numerous decisions on various questions where the standard of conduct applied by the Courts was, " What would a reasonable man have done in the particular circumstances ? " and in none of these decisions will you find that standard anything less than the standard of what may be regarded as the infallible man.

From these decisions you will learn, for example, that no reasonable man when acting as a trustee will ever invest trust money in non-trustee stocks, however good they may be ; no reasonable man in the eyes of the law ever makes a mistake ; no reasonable man ever omits to count the cost or takes a single step without knowing exactly where he is going—in short, he is the perfect man.

In practically all branches of law where it is possible to make a complaint of negligence as a ground of action for reparation or compensation, it is usually possible for the defender not merely to deny that he was negligent but also to put forward a plea that the pursuer himself was the party guilty of negligence or, at least, that the pursuer was guilty of contributory negligence.

Such a plea is, of course, open to any banker against whom such a complaint is made, but it is always a matter for the Court to say on which side lay the negligence which really caused the loss.

One of the earliest outstanding cases dealing with negligence and contributory negligence, and upon which of two negligent parties the loss should fall, is the old case of *Davies* v. *Mann* (1842, 10 Meeson and Welsby 546), where the owner of a donkey had hobbled it and wrongfully turned it on to a public highway to graze. A waggon and team of horses came along driven, as the report says, at a smartish pace and ran into the donkey, which, being hobbled, was unable to save itself and was killed.

The owner of the donkey sued the owner of the waggon for damages on the ground of negligence. The waggon-owner defended the action on the ground of contributory negligence in respect that the donkey ought not to have been let loose on the highway, and, in any event, ought not to have been hobbled. It appeared, however, that the waggon-owner might, with care, have avoided injuring the donkey, and it was held that, although the donkey was wrongfully on the highway and its owner therefore guilty of contributory negligence, the waggon-owner was nevertheless responsible because he might have avoided the accident by taking proper care in driving his waggon and team.

A somewhat similar case in banking law is the well-known case of *London Joint Stock Bank Ltd.* v. *Macmillan & Arthur* (1918, A.C. H.L. 777), which I explained to you when dealing with cheques which had been wrongfully altered or erased. In that case the customers were unsuccessful in their action against the bank, as the Court held that it was the negligence of the customers in filling up the cheque and not the negligence of the bank in paying it which enabled the customers' employee to draw from the customers' bank account a considerably larger sum than that originally represented by the cheque when it was signed.

There are, of course, cases where it is practically impossible to say whether or not the negligence of the pursuer was greater or less than the negligence of the defender, and, where the Court are of opinion that that is the position, they may determine either that the loss should be borne by the parties in given proportions or that it should simply lie where it falls.

I should, however, mention to you that a plea of contributory negligence is more difficult in the case of an action against a collecting banker. It is usually of great force in the case of a claim against a paying banker because there is in such a case a contractual relation between banker and customer involving a duty of care on each to the other. In the case of a collecting banker, however, there is no such contractual relation. Negligence implies a duty and neglect of that duty. A true owner normally owes no duty to a collecting banker, but, on the other hand, the collecting banker owes a duty to the true owner to be careful in his dealings with all the cheques he handles.

The Courts have consistently held that whenever a charge of negligence is made against a collecting banker the onus is on the banker to prove that he has not been negligent. Usually it is for a pursuer to prove his case before he can succeed, but where the defender is a collecting banker charged with negligence the rule is reversed and the defending banker must prove that he is not guilty. In other words, the banker must show that he is entitled to the protection of sec. 82.

Before leaving this short summary of the common and statute law and passing on to individual cases, I should say a word with regard to the prescription of claims of this nature in so far as they may be directed against a banker.

In England the position is fairly clear, because there they have the Statute of Limitations and the Statute of Frauds which do not apply to Scotland and which, generally speaking, put an end to the right of any person to commence an action for redress of this kind after the lapse of six years from the date when the cause of the action first arose.

These Statutes have been successfully pleaded as a defence in quite a number of the actions raised against bankers on the ground of negligence and conversion. In Savory's case, to which I shall refer later, the original sum claimed was, under these Statutes, reduced from £6012 to £5232, 13s. 2d., and in the case of the Carpenters' Co., to which I shall also refer, the original sum claimed was in the same way reduced from £4217 to £1955 because certain of the transactions had taken place more than the six years before.

As regards the position of prescription in Scotland applicable to a claim against a banker on the ground of negligence, the matter is not so clear. Here we have no statute which limits or restricts claims of that nature to those which arise within a limited recent period, and there does not seem to be any decision which deals with the point. Probably it is the long negative prescription of twenty years which is applicable, and, in normal cases, such a long period is useless. In certain claims which I have settled the transactions complained of did not go back more than a comparatively few years, but I could find no authority for contending that any limitation of time applied at all.

There being no reasonably practicable prescription of claims of this nature, the defending banker in Scotland must try something else in order, if possible, to avoid liability, and the alternative usually adopted is to put forward by way of a defence the well-known pleas of *mora* or delay and taciturnity. To succeed on these pleas, however, it is necessary for the banker to show that the claimant was fully aware of his right to make the claims, and, notwithstanding that knowledge, he delayed to do so and held his peace to the prejudice of the defending banker.

That would, I think, be the position of a collecting banker in Scotland who is sued by the true owner on the ground of negligence in handling his cheques. It is quite possible, as disclosed by the last two cases I mentioned, for fraudulent actings to extend over a considerable period without coming to light, and it would only be open to the banker in such a case in Scotland to plead delay or taciturnity when some material time had elapsed after the facts had come to the knowledge of the true owner. To this extent the collecting banker in Scotland appears to be in a much worse position than the collecting banker in England.

There is, however, an additional defence available where a paying banker is being sued by his customer in respect of past transactions. The correctness of the customer's balance is, as you know, specially agreed by him periodically, and the paying banker will no doubt be able to produce the usual signed docquets covering a considerable period of time. These would support the legal doctrine of fitted accounts down, at anyrate, to the date of the last balance, but it is just possible that the transaction which is challenged took place after that date.

Some of the decisions in negligence and conversion cases to which I propose to refer in detail have been mentioned in previous lectures and are already within your cognisance, but I feel justified to some extent in mentioning one or two of them again on the authority of the late J. W. Gilbart, whose name is so familiar in banking circles. In one of his writings he says :—

" In banking, as in other things, we often go astray more from want of firmness than from want of knowledge. We all need to be reminded of a steady adherence to sound principles."

My endeavour in these lectures is accordingly more to emphasise and remind you of the many possible ways in which you may quite unwittingly become involved in a question of negligence and so help you to achieve the position of being not merely good bankers but also, what is much more important in the eyes of the law, reasonable men.

In view of certain recent decisions in England, it would scarcely seem possible to compile a complete list of the various headings under which a charge of negligence may be based, but the more important would appear to include the following :—

Paying a cheque improperly indorsed.—One would have thought that the requisites of an indorsement as called for by sec. 60 were well defined and understood by all concerned, but apparently not. As an illustration of this I would refer you to the case of *Slingsby and Others* v. *The District Bank* (1932, 1 K.B. 544).

The plaintiffs, who were the executors of a Will, kept an account with the District Bank and employed a firm of solicitors, Cumberbirch & Potts, to assist them in matters connected with the trust estate. The acting member of that firm was Mr Cumberbirch, who is described in the report as having been a solicitor of high repute. The plaintiffs, in conference with Cumberbirch, decided to invest through John Prust & Co., their stock-brokers, a sum of £5000, part of the trust estate then on deposit with the bank. Cumberbirch accordingly drew out a form of cheque for signature by the executors. It was in the form " Pay John Prust & Co. or order," and was drawn on the executors' account with the bank. The cheque was signed by the executors and left with Cumber-birch to be posted to the stockbrokers with instructions to invest the money. Cumberbirch, instead of posting the cheque to the stockbrokers, fraudulently inserted the words " per Cumberbirch & Potts " in the blank space between the payees' name and the words " or order." He then indorsed the document with the name " Cumberbirch & Potts " and paid it, so altered and indorsed, into the Westminster Bank to the credit of a company in which he was personally interested and which had an account at that bank. The document was accepted without question by the Westminster Bank and passed through the clearing-house, and the account of the executors with the District Bank was debited, and that of the company with the Westminster Bank was credited, with the amount on the face of the document.

Thereafter several actions were raised in con-nection with the transactions of Cumberbirch, and this was one of them. The executors sued the District Bank as the paying bankers for the amount of their loss on the grounds of conversion, negligence, and breach of duty.

Several points arose for consideration in the

case, and the Court, on appeal, held, as regards
the indorsement in question, that, assuming the
description of the payees " John Prust & Co.
per Cumberbirch & Potts " to be a recognised
although unusual description, the indorsement of
Cumberbirch & Potts alone without any reference
to John Prust & Co. was irregular and invalid
and that the paying bankers were negligent in
honouring the cheque on such a defective indorsement. For this reason the Court held that they
were not entitled to the protection of either sec. 80
or sec. 60.

Quite a number of cheques and dividend warrants
are issued every year in which the payees are
described in some complicated way—such as
" Pay to A. per B. & Co."—and these in practice
are generally paid on the simple indorsement or
signature of B. & Co., without any reference to A.
Obviously that is wrong in view of Slingsby's
case, and the paying banker is accordingly not
protected by sec. 60 in the case of an open cheque,
or by sec. 80 in the case of crossed cheque or
dividend warrant.

The payment of the cheque in that case of
Slingsby, had it been properly indorsed, would
have been protected under the 1882 Act, because
it was a cheque to which the definition in the
Act applied. All the documents which you handle,
however, do not come within the category of a
bill or cheque as defined by that Act, and consequently, in these cases, you have no protection
whatever either as a paying banker or as a collecting
banker.

An illustration of this is to be found in the case
of *Bavins, Jun., & Sims* v. *London & South Western
Bank Ltd.* (1900, 1 Q.B. 270). In that case the
Great Northern Railway Company owed Bavins

a sum of £69, and in settlement sent him one of these composite cheques drawn on the Union Bank of London Ltd. and crossed generally with a receipt form at the foot which required to be signed.

This cheque was stolen from Bavins before it had been indorsed or the receipt form signed, and it was later collected by the London & South Western Bank on behalf of a customer who was unaware of the theft or of the forgery of the payee's signature and indorsement.

On the theft and forgery being discovered, the collecting bankers, the London & South Western Bank, were sued by Bavins, the payee, who was the true owner, and, not having any good answer or protection under any Statute, were held liable for the £69 which the payee had lost.

This composite form of cheque is one which has become quite popular and is used to a considerable extent, but from that case of Bavins you will see the danger which any banker runs who either pays it or collects it. No protection whatever is available to you if anything goes wrong, and the best that you can do as a collecting banker is to see that such cheques, notwithstanding that they are made payable to order, are lodged to the credit of the payee's own account or, if you are the paying banker, paid over to him if you know him, and to no one else. Any mistake, however, will render you liable.

These observations do not apply merely to the banker collecting such a composite cheque. They apply also, as you will see, to the paying banker. In that case of Bavins, the Union Bank of London Ltd., who were the paying bankers, could not at common law have debited payment of the cheque to the account of the drawers, the Great Northern Railway Co., because they had paid away the money without obtaining a proper receipt. They could not be protected by sec. 60 or by sec. 80 as it was not a cheque within the meaning of the 1882 Act, but if they, as paying bankers, had been sued by their customer they might have pleaded sec. 19 of the 1853 Act as the document in question was perhaps a draft or order payable to order on demand. Most of these composite cheques, however, while expressed to be payable to order, are not really so.

While you may be responsible for paying a cheque which has been improperly indorsed, it is also possible that you may be responsible for paying a cheque even when it purports to be properly indorsed.

If, for example, you pay a cheque out of the ordinary course of business, you will not be protected if it turns out that any indorsement on it has been forged. In such a case sec. 60 does not apply at all, and as that section constitutes your only protection in the case of an open cheque, you are left to rely upon the common law, which, as I have already pointed out, says that you are responsible for the validity of all indorsements on the cheques which you pay.

The decision in the case of *Baines* v. *The National Provincial Bank* (1927, 32 Com. Cases 216) allows a banker to deal with a cheque within a reasonable business margin after the advertised time of closing. You must not, however, rely very much upon that case. No definite period is laid down as the length of time after banking hours within which you may safely pay a cheque, and you will keep in view that the considerations which apply to such a payment after hours cannot possibly apply to a payment made before the commencement of the ordinary banking hours.

A similar responsibility may attach to you if you pay a crossed cheque on which one of the indorsements is forged, even although you do so to another banker in terms of the crossing. Sec. 80, you will remember, only protects you where you make such a payment to another banker in good faith and without negligence. To pay a cheque which is improperly indorsed, as was done in the Slingsby case, in itself constitutes negligence, and accordingly involves you in the usual common law responsibility not only for that but for every other defect which can be alleged against the cheque, notwithstanding that the payment is made to another banker.

The validity of the payment of a crossed cheque made in cash across the counter has often been discussed, and views have been expressed that, as the instruction implied by the crossing, not to pay across the counter but to pay to another banker, has been neglected, the paying banker has acted negligently and so made himself responsible for any loss there may be.

That view is undoubtedly correct, but the facts in the particular transaction may be sufficient in themselves to show that this theoretical responsibility has no substance. For example, if the original payee of a crossed cheque who is known to you asks you himself to give him cash across the counter, you will be in safety to do so, but only for the reason that you know definitely that you are paying to the true owner of the cheque on his own indorsement and that, consequently, no other person can allege any loss.

If, however, the person presenting such a crossed cheque at the counter is an indorsee of that cheque, then no matter how well known he may be to you, if you pay cash to him, you do so at your own risk. The reason for this is that while you may know the indorsee presenting the cheque perfectly well and be satisfied as to the genuineness of his indorsement, you do not absolutely know that he is the true owner of the cheque because the preceding indorsement in his favour may have been forged. In such a case the true owner would have a claim against you because you had not complied with the crossing and paid to another banker. You would, of course, have a right of recourse against the person to whom you had paid the money, but that might not give you a great deal of satisfaction.

Paying a cheque which has been altered.— Under sec. 64 it is provided that where a bill is materially altered the bill is avoided, but where the alteration is not apparent, a holder in due course may avail himself of it as if it had not been altered and may enforce payment according to its original tenor.

In the Slingsby case, which I have just mentioned to you, an alteration had been made on the cheque under consideration in respect that Cumberbirch, in whose writing the cheque was, inserted, after it had been signed by the drawers, the words " per Cumberbirch & Potts " in the blank space following the payee's name. That alteration was not and could not be apparent to the paying banker, but the Court held that the cheque had nevertheless been materially altered within the meaning of sec. 64 and that the bank were responsible for the loss under this heading as well as on account of the defective indorsement.

If you will consider sec. 78 you will notice that a crossing is made a material part of a cheque, and it is expressly laid down there that it shall not be lawful for any person to obliterate or, except as authorised by the Act, to add to or to alter a crossing.

The only alterations authorised by the Act to be made on a crossing are those in sec. 77, where it is provided that the holder may cross it generally or specially or add the words "not negotiable." There is no authority whatsoever for obliterating or, if you like, cancelling the crossing, which is definitely said in sec. 78 not to be lawful. Notwithstanding that, however, it is not an uncommon practice for a drawer to cancel the crossing on a cheque which he has issued and to authenticate that cancellation by, it may be, the addition of his initials or signature with or without the words "pay cash."

Such an alteration is an alteration in a material part of the cheque and is not authorised, but, on the contrary, it is expressly laid down as being unlawful. In short, it is not legally possible to convert a crossed cheque into an open cheque. Where any drawer desires to do that, he should use a fresh uncrossed form.

There is a measure of protection given to a banker under sec. 79, but it is a mere shadow, and in practice is of no effect. The banker on whom a crossed cheque is drawn, and who nevertheless pays it otherwise than to another banker, is made liable by subsec. (2) to the true owner for the loss he thereby sustains ; provided—and this is all the protection you can have—that where a cheque is presented for payment which does not appear to be crossed, or to have had a crossing which has been obliterated, the paying banker does not incur any liability if he acts in good faith and without negligence.

That is to say, if there is no evidence on the face of the cheque that it had once been crossed, then you may safely pay it over the counter. But if there is any obliterated crossing on the cheque or any evidence that it once was crossed, you must deal with it as if it still were crossed. In other words, a crossed cheque can never be converted into an open cheque—not even by the drawer.

Take, as an example of this, the common wages cheque. As often as not, this is payable to Selves or to the named cashier or other messenger, and probably has a printed crossing which has been obliterated or cancelled, or has the words "ignore crossing" or "pay cash" added. If the money you pay over the counter for such a cheque disappears in any way, you will be liable for the loss, because, notwithstanding the alterations on the cheque, however authenticated, you have paid a cheque which is still a crossed cheque otherwise than to a banker. In such a case payment is not being made to the true owner, but to an ostensible agent.

You will naturally think it very hard if you are called upon to meet a claim under such circumstances, and you must keep in mind that the claim may not be made by your customer but by his insurance company, who had issued to him a bond guaranteeing the fidelity of his employees and who now take his place in the matter. Or the claim may be made at a later date by a liquidator of your customer if a limited company or a trustee in bankruptcy in the case of an individual.

Your only answers to such a claim would be precedent following upon a long-established practice, and, failing that, contributory negligence. As regards the plea of established practice you would probably be met with the rule of law that the continuation or repetition of a wrong does not convert it into a right, and as regards contributory negligence your case would not be strong because, like the waggon-owner I told you about, you could have avoided the loss by refusing to pay in such an irregular way.

This is clearly another instance where the banker should contract out of his legal liability and either insist upon unaltered open cheques being used for wages or, alternatively, upon obtaining a separate indemnity from any customer who will not use such cheques for this purpose.

There are other cases involving negligence where payment would appear to be all in order, but where on careful consideration that cannot really be said to be the case. All cheques in ordinary circumstances are considered to be negotiable, and, on being indorsed in blank by the payee, are equivalent to bearer cheques and capable of being passed from hand to hand.

This, however, is subject to qualification by reason of the fact that any banker, whether paying or collecting, has, at common law, a duty to see that he is not involved in the fraudulent change over of the property of A. into the property of B. That brings us to the next class of cases.

Paying a cheque which operates conversion.— This class requires several cases to be quoted in order to enable you to appreciate the various dangers requiring to be guarded against.

In *Phillips* v. *The Italian Bank Ltd.* (1934, S.L.T. 78) a commercial traveller, whose business it was to collect cash and cheques from his employers' customers in settlement of their debts, obtained from these customers various cheques drawn in favour of his employers, a limited company, some of which were crossed and some uncrossed.

Without the knowledge of his employers, the traveller indorsed each of these cheques with the name of his employers, adding thereto his own signature. He then presented them to the Italian Bank, who had only one office, and received payment in cash over the counter in each case. The employers, on discovering what had been going on, raised an action against the bank for payment of the sums in the cheques so cashed by their traveller.

In addition to sundry other pleas, the bank pled that they were entitled to the protection afforded under the 1882 Act. The Court, however, held that as regards the uncrossed cheques the bank were not entitled to the protection of sec. 60 as paying bankers because the indorsements put on these uncrossed cheques by the traveller were not the indorsements of or purporting to be made by the payee in the sense of the section.

Lord Wark, in his judgment, said : " In considering the indorsement, it has to be kept in view that the payee of each of the cheques was a Limited Company. The proper method of indorsement of such a cheque would be, ' For or on behalf of or per procuration of the Company ' by one of its officials with the addition of his official designation —*e.g.*, as Manager or Secretary. Such an indorsement would have been sufficient to protect the defenders."

With all deference, I cannot accept Lord Wark's opinion as to the effect of any such indorsement, and I shall deal further with that point. I agree, however, that Lord Wark was quite correct in holding that the indorsement in this last particular case was irregular, and, that being so, the paying bankers, like the paying bankers in Slingsby's case, were held liable. You will therefore keep in view that sec. 60 is of no use to you if the indorsement on any cheque you pay is not in a regular and proper form. It is not in the ordinary course of business to pay on an irregular indorsement.

As regards the crossed cheques in that Italian Bank case, the bank were held not to be entitled to claim the protection of sec. 60 or sec. 80 for the reason that the indorsements were irregular, and they do not appear to have pled, even assuming it were competent, that they were entitled to the protection of sec. 82, probably for the reason that they were not collecting the cheques on behalf of a customer.

Sec. 79 (2), you will remember, provides that where a banker on whom a crossed cheque is drawn pays otherwise than to a banker, he is liable to the true owner of the cheque for any loss sustained owing to the cheque having been so paid. As the crossed cheques in the Italian Bank case were paid over the counter in cash and not to a banker, the Court held that the true owners of these cheques—*i.e.,* the payees—were entitled to recover their loss from the bank.

Another case under somewhat similar circumstances is that of the *Carpenters' Livery Co.* v. *The British Mutual Banking Co. Ltd.* (53 T.L.R. 1040). In that case an employee of the Carpenters' Co., by means of misrepresentation and/or other inducement, obtained delivery of cheques drawn by the Carpenters' Co. in favour of certain tradesmen who were said to have supplied goods to them, but who, as a matter of fact, had not done so. All these cheques were crossed. The employee forged the indorsements of these tradesmen and lodged the cheques to the credit of his own private account with the same bank. In this case also the bank had only one office.

The bank, knowing that the employee was a servant of their other customers, the Carpenters' Co., asked him why he was paying these tradesmen's cheques to the credit of his own account, and he plausibly explained that as he had already paid the tradesmen out of his own pocket pending the signature of the cheques, he was therefore entitled to ask that the cheques should be credited to his account.

In this case the bank put forward the defence that they were merely paying bankers and were accordingly protected by sec. 60 or by sec. 80 of the Act, but the Court held that these sections only applied where the banker was merely acting as a paying banker and that they do not apply where any element of collection comes in. Accordingly, a banker acting in such a dual capacity cannot rely upon these sections—60 and 80—but must bring himself within sec. 82 as a collecting banker. Inasmuch as the bank failed to show that they had acted without negligence in this case in continuing a wrongful practice over a period of some fifteen years and crediting an employer's cheques for large sums to the account of an employee, the bank were not within sec. 82 and were, therefore, liable.

In some cases where suitable circumstances are present it may be possible for a collecting banker who has dealt with the collection of a crossed cheque, whether negligently or not, on behalf of a customer to take up the position that he is a holder in due course. To be a holder in due course in terms of sec. 29, the banker only requires to show that he had taken the cheque in good faith and for value and without notice of any defect in the title of the person who negotiated it to him. If he can do that, then sec. 82 or the fact that he may have been negligent does not need to worry him, as he can sue on the cheque just as an ordinary holder would be entitled to do.

This assumes, of course, that there is no suggestion of a forged indorsement. Collection of a crossed cheque bearing a forged indorsement is protected by sec. 82, but where a claim is being made by a holder in due course where one of the indorsements is forged, his position is bad because, as you know, there can be no legal holder under a forged signature.

This leads on to an interesting question which is difficult to answer, and that is : Can a paying banker claim to be a holder for value or a holder in due course of a cheque drawn on him by one of his own customers ? The circumstances under which such a question may be raised are varied, and it will be quite interesting for you to speculate as to what is the correct legal position.

Some of these various sets of circumstances may, for example, be as follows :—

1. Where the paying banker has inadvertently debited his customer's account with a cheque of which payment had been duly countermanded ;
2. Where the amount of the cheque is credited to the payee's account at one branch while the drawer's account is kept at a different branch of the same bank ;
3. Where the banker has paid a cheque bearing several successive indorsements while the sum at the drawer's credit was insufficient to meet the cheque in full.

In considering that somewhat nice question you will no doubt keep in view what was said in the case of *Coats* v. *The Union Bank of Scotland Ltd.* (1929, S.C. H.L. 114) as to the legal effect of a cheque after being debited by the paying banker to his customer's account. Such a document in that case was no longer a negotiable instrument in a question with the drawers as regards joint and several liability, but was merely a voucher proving the payment of the money. You will also keep in view the difficulty of a paying banker suing his own customer on a cheque in the guise of a holder thereof in due course, when he should perhaps be suing simply for payment of the debit balance and using the cheque as one of the vouchers to instruct the payment.

LECTURE II.

THE relationship of banker and customer is a very important one and involves in many cases such far-reaching consequences that I would like to deal with that for a little before passing on to specific examples of negligence arising out of relationship.

There is no statutory definition of the word ' customer,' but it has now come to imply certain important qualifications which we shall deal with later.

The only definition of the word ' banker ' is that contained in the Bills of Exchange Act of 1882, where it is defined as including a body of persons, whether incorporated or not, who carry on the business of banking. Such a definition is, of course, quite useless and might quite well have been omitted from the Act altogether.

There is a number of cases in the books, however, in which consideration has been given to the question as to who is a banker and who is a customer, and, like decisions in connection with many other points in banking, these are neither clear nor consistent.

So far as one can make out from the general tenor of the opinions of the various Judges which have been recorded in these cases, it is necessary to look closely at the business relationship between the so-called banker on the one hand and the so-called customer on the other. The word ' customer,' as you know, is used in the 1882 Act, but has no definition attached to it. You will find it in sec. 82, where a collecting banker is protected when he handles a crossed cheque, provided that he is collecting it for a customer.

Such a customer must, of course, be a banker's customer, and it is therefore necessary to ascertain in the first place who may be regarded as a banker, and from that who may be regarded as a banker's customer.

There are many forms of activity in which the banks of to-day take part, but some of these forms of activity are also carried on by other concerns which could not possibly be referred to as banks.

For example, the acceptance of money on deposit at interest repayable either on demand or on notice is business which is done by various kinds of finance and investment concerns and cannot be regarded as banking. On the other hand, the lending of money at interest repayable on demand or on notice is also carried on by other concerns which cannot be regarded as banks. The same observations apply to dealings in foreign currencies and sundry other useful services undertaken by other concerns as well as by banks.

Having regard, however, to the general terms of the 1882 Act, one comes to the conclusion that there is one special form of activity the carrying on of which alone entitles a person to call himself a banker. That is the borrowing or receipt of money on a current account repayable on demand by means of cheques or drafts or orders issued from time to time by the party from whom such money has been received or borrowed. If you take away that form of activity from any of the concerns which we have in view, they would at once cease to be banks and become ordinary finance or investment corporations.

Having thus come to the conclusion that a banker is a person who receives money on current account operated upon by cheque, it follows that his customer must be a person who keeps such a current account with that banker.

Turning for a moment to one aspect of the business relationship of a banker and his customer, where the existence of a current account is not necessarily an essential, I would like to quote to you two cases of negligence in matters which are usually dealt with by bankers. The first is that of *Holt & Co.* v. *Markham* (1923, 1 K.B. 504).

Holt & Co., as you know, acted as the Agents of the Government for the payment of gratuities to demobilised officers of the Air Force, and, in pursuance of their duties in that connection, they paid over to Markham a gratuity of £744. In doing so, they appeared to be in ignorance of the fact that Markham was on an Emergency List of officers, and also to have forgotten a regulation which provided that gratuities to officers on that list were payable at a lower rate than the normal. They accordingly had overpaid him by £310. This was pointed out by the Air Ministry to the bank about a year later when the accounts were audited, and the excess payment was disallowed by the Air Ministry.

Thereupon the bank endeavoured to recover the excess payment from Markham as money paid to him under a mistake in fact. By that time Markham had spent the money and he refused to admit any legal liability to repay.

The Court of Appeal held that, as Markham had been led by the conduct of the bank in making the payment to believe that he might treat the money as his own, and that as he had in that belief altered his position by spending the money, the bank were estopped from alleging that they had paid the money under a mistake in fact.

The decision in a previous case of *Skyring* v. *Greenwood* (4 B. and C. 281) was referred to, and the following passage from the opinion of one of the Judges quoted with approval: " It is of great importance to any man, and certainly not less to military men than others, that they should not be led to suppose that their annual income is greater than it really is. Every prudent man accommodates his mode of living to what he supposes to be his income ; it therefore works a great prejudice to any man if, after having had credit given him in account for certain sums, and having been allowed to draw on his agent on the faith that those sums belonged to him, he may be called upon to pay them back."

It is somewhat difficult to reconcile this decision with others relating to the rule as to payments made on a mistake in fact. This was not a case, as the Court appeared to assume, of a person erroneously enjoying an income which did not really belong to him and which, when spent, cannot be recovered. That, I agree, would be good law if it had been a question of income or the annual fruits of an estate or investment, but the sum dealt with here was of the nature of a capital or at anyrate special and non-recurring nature to which the ordinary rule as to payment on mistake in fact ought normally to apply. The decision, as it stands, however, is a warning to you of the danger you may run if you should even unwittingly pass credits to the account of a customer who has no legal right to them.

The other somewhat special case I have in mind is that of *Gowers* v. *Lloyds & National Provincial Foreign Bank Ltd.* (53 T.L.R. 713).

This was an action by the Crown Agents for the Colonies against the bank claiming the recovery of £3502, 2s. 8d. as money had and received to their use or money paid under a mistake in fact.

In 1907 a Mr Gibson, who had been an officer in the Customs Service in Mauritius, retired on pension and settled in France, and from 1916 onwards he collected his pension from the Crown Agents through the bank. From 1926 the pension was paid by the bank by post on the receipt of certain receipt forms, which purported to be signed by Gibson and also by one Michel Matteix, a doctor of medicine. In 1935 Gibson's wife died, and it was then discovered that Gibson had himself died in 1929, and that since that date the receipt forms had been forged.

The Crown Agents claimed that the bank had impliedly warranted that they had authority to collect the pension on behalf of Gibson and that the bank were, therefore, liable to repay to the Crown Agents the amount wrongfully obtained from them.

The Court held, however, that there was no warranty to be implied on the part of the bank to the effect that Gibson was still living, as the bank themselves had not given any certificate to that effect, and that accordingly the money could not be recovered from them by the Crown Agents.

This decision also is somewhat difficult to reconcile with others where it has been laid down that an Agent is responsible for the validity of documents put forward by him and acted upon in good faith by the party receiving them. I refer to the legal principle which has been applied, for example, in the case of an agent presenting a forged transfer of stock or shares to a company for registration, and later on I would like to explain this to you further.

So far as the customer is concerned, it is usually of little moment to him with which banker he deals. Under ordinary circumstances he can select any banker he pleases and can change about from time to time to suit his own requirements.

The position of the banker, however, is somewhat different because, in the first place, the hazard of selection, as they say in insurance circles, is against him. Only in very isolated cases is a banker in a position to pick and choose as to which customers he shall put on his books. The exigencies of modern business, coupled with a quite unnecessary element of competition, practically oblige every banker to take on as a customer any person who has the appearance of being able to provide even the most modest amount of new business.

If the banker in his anxiety to add to his new business omits to remember what the law will require him to show at a later date in the event of anything going wrong, he will place himself at a serious disadvantage. The general conception held by the Courts of a banker's position as disclosed by many recent cases is that he is responsible not only for his own actings but for the actings of his customers. Generally speaking, the Courts, in effect, seem to take the view that a banker holds himself and his customers up to the whole world as being persons with whom anyone may deal in perfect safety. In other words, the banker is expected to be responsible not only for his own integrity and his own actings, but also for the reliability, honesty and respectability of his customers.

It is consequently of the utmost importance, particularly when the hazard of selection is against you, that you should take every precaution to see that you are not accepting or retaining a customer about whose dealings there may be the slightest question. You will be expected to be able to show that you knew all about your customer and his affairs and connections not only in relation to his private matters, but also in relation to his business or employment or his associations with other people.

By way of illustration of this aspect of your position I would refer you to the case of *Ladbroke* v. *Todd* (1914, 30 T.L.R. 433). In that case the plaintiffs, who were a firm of bookmakers, had posted to one of their successful clients a cheque in settlement of his winnings. That cheque was drawn on the National Bank in favour of the payee or order and crossed " Account payee."

Unfortunately a thief managed to extract the letter containing that cheque from the pillar-box in which it had been posted, and, having fraudulently indorsed the payee's name upon it, took it to the defender who was carrying on the John Bull Bank and opened an account by paying in the amount of the cheque for that purpose. The bank were apparently satisfied by their new customer's appearance and deportment and did not think it necessary to make any enquiries about him.

The thief told the bank that he was desirous of having the cheque cleared at once, and the bank were so obliging as to get that done the same day. The next day the thief drew on the account for the amount of the cheque which had been credited to him. Shortly afterwards the fraud was discovered when the plaintiffs, the bookmakers, issued to their client another cheque in settlement of his winnings, taking from him at the same time an assignment of his claims against the bank for the loss of the amount of the first cheque on the ground of their negligence. The plaintiffs, as such assignees, thereupon sued the bank for negligence, while the bank claimed the protection of sec. 82 on the ground that they had collected the cheque on behalf of a customer.

The Court found as a fact that, although the bank had received payment of the cheque in good faith, they had not taken reasonable precautions to safeguard the interests of persons who might be the true owners of the cheque and therefore could not claim the protection of the section. The Court expressed the opinion that the bank would have been entitled to the protection of sec. 82 as having received the payment on behalf of a customer, but that they had deprived themselves of the right to that protection by their want of due care in satisfying themselves by proper enquiry as to the identity and *bona fides* of their customer.

In that case you will notice that the bank took no steps at all to investigate the position or character of their new customer, but here is another case where the bank did take steps to that end but which turned out to be insufficient. In the case of *The Guardians of St John's, Hampstead* v. *Barclays Bank Ltd.* (1923, 39 T.L.R. 229) a stranger called at the bank to open an account, giving his name as Donald Stewart, with an address in Fitzroy Square, London. The bank, not knowing the gentleman, asked him for a reference, and were given the name and address of a Mr Woolfe, of whom the bank also knew nothing. A small payment was there and then made to the credit of the account, but the bank declined to issue a cheque-book until they had verified the reference which had been given. Thereupon they communicated with Mr Woolfe, and, in reply, received a satisfactory answer confirming that the new customer was a person of respectability and responsibility. That reply could not have been anything else but satisfactory, as it unfortunately turned out later on to have been forged.

Later this customer called and lodged to the credit of his account certain cheques or orders drawn in favour of D. Stewart & Co., and explained to the bank that that was the name under which he carried on business and that these cheques represented payments of certain business accounts due to him. The bank accepted these cheques and placed them to the credit of the new account which they had opened in the name of Donald Stewart. They, however, omitted to notice or did not realise the significance of the fact that these cheques were dated some twenty-three days previously. Later Stewart obtained a cheque-book from the bank in the usual way and drew out all the money which had been so placed to his credit, and disappeared.

In the action raised subsequently by the plaintiffs against the bank, the bank endeavoured to obtain the protection of sec. 82 in respect that they had collected the cheques in question on behalf of a customer, but the Court held that the bank had been negligent in failing to verify the reference which they had received from Woolfe. If that had been done they would have discovered that the reference was not genuine. From this it follows that your duty does not end when you receive what might appear to be a satisfactory reference or a satisfactory explanation. Unless you have good reason to believe that these are actually true, then you must proceed to test the truth of them. You must not merely take them on trust.

The Court also held in that case that the bank were negligent in allowing cheques drawn in favour of D. Stewart & Co. to be credited to an account in name of Donald Stewart without being satisfied as to the absolute right of Stewart to have these cheques placed to his own personal credit. The mere fact that the cheques had been dated twenty-three days before they were lodged to the credit of that account should also have led the bank to suspect that all was not well.

Apart from the negligence on the part of the bank in that case in failing to make proper enquiries as to their customer, the decision once more emphasises how a cheque or order which, on the face of it, is freely negotiable may not really be so. As you know, the general belief is that, where a cheque which bears to be payable to order, without any specialty such as " Account payee," &c., and has been properly indorsed by the payee in blank, that cheque becomes a bearer cheque and is capable of being passed from hand to hand. Strictly speaking, however, that is not so. While it may be good enough as a general rule, you cannot follow it in safety in every case or, indeed, in any case, unless you are thoroughly satisfied that you are dealing with the true owner.

I have already mentioned the case of *Underwood* v. *The Bank of Liverpool and Martins* (1924, 1 K.B. 775), where the sole director of a limited company held the whole issued capital of £10,000 with the exception of one share of £1 held by a colleague of his in order to comply with the Companies Acts. This director, who was the ostensible owner of the whole business, indorsed cheques drawn in favour of his limited company in quite the correct manner, thereby making them to all intents and purposes bearer cheques, but, instead of paying them to the credit of the company's bank account, he paid them to the credit of his own private account.

On the death of that director, a receiver and manager of the company was appointed by the debenture holders, and, after the affairs of the limited company had been investigated by him, an action was raised against the bank for repayment of the amount of the cheques which had been credited to the director's personal account instead of to an account in name of the company. Again the bank pleaded the protection of sec. 82 as having collected the cheques on behalf of a customer in good faith and without negligence, but the Court appeared to have little difficulty in holding that the bank were negligent in allowing a limited company's cheques to be credited to a director's own personal account and that this resulted in conversion, which gave rise to a good claim against them.

One other similar case is that of *Alexander Stewart & Son, of Dundee, Limited* v. *The Westminster Bank* (1926, W.N. 271). The circumstances there were very nearly the same as those in Underwood's case, and the bank were held liable for the limited company's loss because they could not say under sec. 82 that they had acted without negligence in giving a director credit for cheques which, on the face of them, were originally the property of the limited company although indorsed in such a form as to make them otherwise practically bearer cheques.

You will therefore gather that it is a somewhat delicate matter for you to handle cheques drawn payable to any particular payee and presented to you by some third party unless you are thoroughly satisfied as to that third party being the true owner of such cheques. You must not rely upon the apparent negotiability of the documents.

For example, in the case of a cheque drawn payable to a limited company, the ownership of that cheque is plainly shown on the face of it, and, as I have said, you must not be misled by the fact that it is drawn payable to order or that it is uncrossed and therefore apparently negotiable.

Limited companies are the creatures of statute, and, owing to their nature, are unable to act by themselves. Everything they do must be done for them by directors or other officials, and when a limited company open a bank account the only method whereby they can operate on that account is by means of cheques signed by their directors or officials on their behalf. Accordingly, the instructions to the banker as to how the company's account is to be dealt with are given in a Minute passed by their authorised directors setting forth what the arrangements are to be.

Whenever an account is opened in name of a limited company the banker, therefore, in every case takes care to see that he is furnished with a copy of the company's Memorandum and Articles of Association and a certified excerpt from the Minutes of the directors who have been authorised to act on behalf of the company.

In that Minute instructions are specifically given to the banker as to how the cheques drawing money out of the account are to be signed on behalf of the company, and also, in many cases, how cheques drawn in favour of the company are to be indorsed. If any instructions are so given with regard to indorsements, these invariably bear that such indorsements are only to be valid for the purpose of enabling the cheques to be lodged to the credit of the company's account.

If the Minute is silent as to the method to be employed in the indorsement of the company's cheques, then you are entirely without instructions on that point, but if the cheques are being credited to the company's account you cannot go wrong even although the indorsement has been put on, say, by a cashier.

I do not think you will find any such Minute among your records authorising you to pay in cash across the counter any cheque drawn payable to or indorsed in favour of a limited company. If an uncrossed cheque drawn payable to a limited company is presented to you for payment in cash across the counter, then, no matter how well that cheque is indorsed, you will not be in safety in paying cash for it unless the Minute which you hold expressly authorises you to do so. The reason for this is that the true owner, that is the company, is not the person demanding the money at the counter, who is merely a servant or messenger, and you are entirely without authority to pay to him. In the absence of express instructions you must assume that the amount of the cheque in question was intended by the company to be credited to their account.

The same remarks apply in the case of a bearer cheque. If a cheque is presented to you for payment which is drawn payable to a limited company or bearer, then under no circumstances will you be in safety to pay that cheque in cash across the counter unless your Minute expressly authorises you to do so. Generally speaking, you may take it that cheques drawn payable to or indorsed in favour of a limited company are not negotiable notwithstanding their terms.

These observations in connection with cheques drawn payable to or indorsed in favour of a limited company apply with equal force to cheques drawn payable to firms and other similar associations. You cannot, for example, justify crediting the personal account of a partner of a firm with a cheque drawn payable to his firm. If he is to your absolute knowledge, however, the sole partner of that firm, then possibly you cannot go far wrong, but it may be a very difficult matter for you if any question is afterwards raised to prove that that partner was the sole partner of that firm and had the absolute right to have that cheque credited to his own private account.

You will therefore realise that as a general rule the handling of what might be termed third party cheques is fraught with difficulty if not with danger to you, and every instance of such a transaction should be properly enquired into before it is put through. That, of course, is in your own interests and for your own protection, but there is something even more than that in it. For example, if a customer of yours wishes to place to the credit of his account with you a cheque drawn payable to a third party and indorsed by that third party to your customer, then, apart from your own interest in seeing that matters are right, your customer may be grateful to you if you were to draw his attention to the risk which he himself may be running.

In the case of Bavins, to which I referred in the previous lecture, you will remember that the customer who lodged a third party's cheque to the credit of his account was unaware that that cheque had been stolen, and he was also unaware that the previous indorsement had been forged. Apart from these risks your customer may not be aware that for him to take payment of a debt by means of an indorsed cheque is not a payment in the ordinary course of business within the meaning of the 1696 Act.

You will no doubt recall the case of *Carter* v. *Johnstone* (1886, 13 R. 698), where a man, within the sixty days preceding his bankruptcy, had indorsed a cheque on which he was the payee and handed it to one of his creditors in payment of a past due debt. The Court of Session held that such indorsement and delivery of the cheque were reducible under the 1696 Act as being neither a cash payment nor a transaction in the ordinary course of business, and therefore reducible. In such a case the money must be handed back to the bankrupt's trustee in full and a ranking for a dividend thereon accepted instead.

If, therefore, any customer who wishes to lodge a third party's cheque to the credit of his own account feels dissatisfied with your objection to his doing so, as may not infrequently be the case, you will no doubt be able to satisfy him that it is his own position under the 1696 Act and his own interest that you are endeavouring to protect.

It is not only in connection with the opening of an account that you may become involved in a question of negligence. It is, in the view which the Courts have taken as to the position which a banker and his customers are supposed to occupy, your duty to see that the operations on an account are not only free from suspicious transactions but are in keeping with the class of business or the style and position of your customer. If you fail to appreciate the possible significance of the entries which are passing through any particular customer's account, you may perhaps expose yourselves to a charge of negligence at the instance of some third party who suffers loss owing in some way to your customer's banking transactions.

In the case of *The Clydesdale Bank Ltd.* v. *The Continental Chocolate Co.* (1917) the bank raised an action against three partners of a firm who had opened an account with them on which it had been arranged that cheques might be drawn by any one of these three partners. One of these partners overdrew the account and the other two partners denied liability for the overdraft. Their defence was that the cheques which were challenged were drawn by one of the partners for a purpose apparently not connected with the firm's ordinary course of business, that the bank were aware of that, and that they had no reasonable ground for believing that that partner had power to bind the firm on the particular cheques in question.

The Court, however, held that the defenders had failed to establish the defence which they put forward. That decision, of course, was arrived at on the basis of the facts put before the Court in that particular case, but it must be kept in view in every case that the operations on a firm's bank account require close scrutiny on your part if you are to avoid similar questions being raised with you.

On the other hand, apart from the particular nature of the operations on the account, if these operations appear to be of an abnormal character having regard to your customer's circumstances, it will be necessary for you to look closely into the matter. In this connection I would like to emphasise that, while you may be charged with negligence as regards only one particular cheque and while you may be able to show that you did not act negligently as regards that cheque, you may not be able to show that you are altogether clear of negligence as regards the general conduct of your customer's account. If you have not taken the necessary care to see that the operations on the account in general are in keeping with your customer's position and business, the imputation of negligence will not be confined to the payment or collection of the one cheque which has been challenged.

In this connection I would merely refer you to the decisions in *Crumplin* v. *The London Joint Stock Bank* (30 T.L.R. 99), *Morison* v. *The London County and Westminster Bank* (1914, 3 K.B. 356), and *Lloyds Bank* v. *The Chartered Bank of India, Australia and China* (1929, 1 K.B. 40). In the last-mentioned case fraudulent transactions were being carried on by an employee who was, by certain roundabout means, placing to the credit of his own individual account sums of money belonging to his employers. The defending bank in that case were held responsible for negligence and conversion. Mr Justice MacKinnon partly based his judgment on the payment by the employee of large cheques to the credit of his private account and the failure on the part of the bank to make enquiry as to the regularity of these transactions. The Court of Appeal adopted that finding, and added that an examination of the employee's account (and they were sure that general examination of the account of every customer takes place from time to time in all well-managed banks) should have put the defending bankers on enquiry as to the source from which these heavy payments were being made, particularly in the case of an account which was generally in low water except for these payments-in which were immediately reduced by payments-out.

Even although the operations which take place on your customer's account may appear to be satisfactory, your customer's method of dealing with his banking transactions always requires your consideration. Quite a number of customers from time to time issue cheques which cannot be paid when presented owing to the lack of funds, and it is very unsatisfactory to any banker to have to return such a cheque unpaid. It detracts from the banker's own prestige that he should have such a customer on his books in the possession of a cheque-book and using it and the good name of the bank as well to disappoint that customer's creditors. Particularly is this so in the case of special cheques, that is, cheques which are specially prepared with the customer's name printed thereon. It is bad enough to see an ordinary form of cheque returned marked R/D, but it is very much worse to see one of these special cheques so returned. The very fact that the bank have gone to the expense of printing a special cheque for any customer should carry with it a certain amount of weight in the eyes of parties accepting these cheques, and it is all the more disappointing to have such a cheque returned unpaid.

It is, therefore, not only good practice for you to deal in a suitable manner with any of your customers who issue cheques when they have good reason to believe that they will not be paid, but, in so doing, you will maintain your own high position in business circles and, in addition, you will minimise the possibility of a claim of negligence from some outsider.

It is perhaps a little difficult to appreciate that a customer who issues cheques which are returned by you marked R/D is not a suitable customer for you to have, but that is the fact. He is a danger to you, and you should take the first opportunity of closing his account.

I have one example of this to give to you for your serious consideration. It is the case of *The Motor Traders' Guarantee Corporation Ltd.* v. *The Midland Bank Ltd.* (54 T.L.R. 10). In that case the Motor Traders' business included the financing of hire-purchase agreements. In one of these transactions they agreed to buy a car from certain dealers, Welch & Co., for one Turner, and they drew a cheque on their account at Lloyds Bank for £189, 5s. in favour of the dealers and handed that cheque to Turner in exchange for the signed documents—the understanding being that Turner would hand the cheque to the dealers in exchange for the car.

Turner, however, forged the indorsement of the payees, Welch & Co., and paid the cheque to the credit of his account with the Midland Bank. The proceeds were duly collected by that bank.

The Midland Bank teller, when he took in that cheque, noticed that it was a third party cheque— that is, one drawn payable to Welch & Co. and by them indorsed in favour of Turner, their customer. He accordingly asked Turner how he came to be paying such a cheque into the credit of his own account. Turner replied that the amount formed part of money due to him by the payees, Welch & Co., and that this was their way of settling it. The teller knew from looking at the ledger that Welch & Co., the payees, and Turner, the indorsee, had had business transactions before relating to motor-cars, and he felt satisfied with the explanation.

The fraud, of course, was discovered, and the

drawers of the cheque, The Motor Traders' Guarantee Corporation, sued the Midland Bank for loss on the ground of negligence and conversion, and the bank pleaded in reply that they were protected by sec. 82 in respect that they had acted in good faith and without negligence and had collected the cheque on behalf of a customer.

The bank tried to argue that this case was quite different from any of the others previously reported, in respect that Turner, their customer, was an independent person altogether and was not a servant of the drawers of the cheque or of the payees. They also argued that, whereas in other cases the collecting banker had made no enquiries as to the cheque, they had, as a matter of fact, questioned Turner and had received a reasonable explanation as to why a third party cheque was going to the credit of his account.

Mr Justice Goddard, in giving judgment, admitted that during the hearing his mind had fluctuated as to where the responsibility should eventually fall, and that, but for one fact, he would have decided in favour of the bank and given them the protection of sec. 82.

During the hearing of the case it had been disclosed that in the six months during which Turner's account had been in existence numerous cheques had been issued, but of these thirty-five had been returned dishonoured. Some undoubtedly had been paid subsequently, but others had not been paid at all.

Mr Justice Goddard went on to say that if Turner's banking antecedents had been satisfactory, the explanation which he gave to the teller with regard to the cheque in question would have justified the bank, but, because these antecedents had not been satisfactory, then, for that reason and for that reason only, his Lordship held that the bank had not discharged the onus laid on them by sec. 82 of showing that they had acted without negligence.

You will therefore see that an unsatisfactory customer of this kind who issues cheques which are not paid when presented is a real danger to you. All your actings may have been conducted in good faith and without negligence, and after making the appropriate enquiries and receiving satisfactory answers; nevertheless, if your customer issues cheques which cannot be paid, you will be responsible for his fraudulent banking transactions. It is for you to see that no customer of yours makes an improper use of his bank account or his cheque-book.

You are not to think that the Courts in the decisions quoted to you in these Lectures and elsewhere have put a strained interpretation on secs. 60, 80 and 82, or have expanded the basis of a banker's liabilities. All that the Courts have done is to apply the rules of common law which I explained to you in my first lecture and which call for careful conduct on the part of every citizen with the view of avoiding loss being knowingly caused to another.

The 1882 Act does not set forth the law of negligence of bankers at all. That law is to be found somewhere else altogether. The Act must be read along with and as an addition to the common law and not, as banks and their advisers in some cases appear to have thought, as a separate code by itself excluding all rules of law not expressly incorporated in it.

If, therefore, you wish to know what the law is as regards liability for negligence in the conduct of your business, you must not look at the 1882

Act but at the various well-known books on negligence and the principles and decisions therein explained. When you have done that you may then turn to the Act to see whether it contains for you any exemption from such liability in the special circumstances of the transaction you may have under consideration at the moment.

In the previous Lecture I gave you a short outline of the common law rules relating to negligence, and my quotation of the various cases with which we have dealt is for the purpose of illustrating and bringing home to you the practical application of these rules of common law and to show that the immunities conferred by the 1882 Act did not alter these rules in any way.

I think that on full reflection on this aspect of your position you will agree that the decisions of the Court, however strained they might appear to be in some cases, were not so very far wrong, and that what is wrong is that the immunities conferred by the Act are not wide enough for your purposes.

LECTURE III.

In this Lecture I would like to continue dealing with negligence and responsibility on the part of bankers from some aspects differing from those previously dealt with.

You will recollect that in the previous Lecture I mentioned to you the case of *Gowers* v. *Lloyds & National Provincial Foreign Bank Ltd.* where the bank, as agents for a colonial official who had retired and was living in France during the latter part of his lifetime, delivered to the Crown Agents for the Colonies receipts for the official's pension and, in exchange, collected the sums due in name of pension.

From the legal point of view the bank, as agents for the pensioner, just like any other agent, would normally be deemed to warrant to the Crown Agents that they were actually representing the pensioner and that the receipts delivered by them were valid and legal. Instead of that, however, the bank during the latter years were actually, although in ignorance, purporting to represent a man who had died, and not only that but were purporting to deliver as valid legal receipts documents which had been forged apparently by the pensioner's widow.

You will recollect that the bank were found not to be liable to repay the amount of pension

251

thus erroneously collected by them, as the Court took the view that they had not warranted that the pensioner was alive or that the receipts were properly signed. That decision, if not exactly contradictory to certain previous decisions of the House of Lords, is very difficult indeed to reconcile therewith, and, as the responsibility of a bank when acting as agents is of importance to you, I thought it as well to deal with your position in such a connection.

The general rule of law is that any person who holds himself out as an agent representing a principal is deemed to warrant to all parties dealing with him that he has been duly authorised so to act and also that the documents which he delivers, bearing to be executed by his principal, have in fact been so executed.

An important phase of a banker's business in this respect is the handling of transfers of stocks and shares and the presentation of such transfers to the various companies for registration in their books.

One important case which is of great interest to bankers in this connection is that of *Starkey* v. *Bank of England* (1903, A.C. 114).

The facts in that case were that a sum of consols was standing inscribed in the books of the Bank of England in the joint names of F. W. Oliver and his brother, Edgar Oliver. F. W. Oliver wrote to a firm of stockbrokers, of which Starkey was a partner, enclosing an application addressed to the Bank of England, requesting them to issue a Power of Attorney from F. W. Oliver and Edgar Oliver in favour of Starkey in order to transfer the consols, and requested the brokers to lodge the application with the bank.

That application having been lodged by Starkey

with the Bank of England, the bank thereupon issued to him a form of Power of Attorney to sell and transfer the consols and, at the same time, sent notices of their having done so to both F. W. Oliver and Edgar Oliver at the addresses given in the bank's books. The notice addressed to Edgar Oliver, however, did not reach him.

Starkey then forwarded the Power of Attorney to F. W. Oliver, who had written to him on the subject, and he thereupon returned it to the brokers executed by himself and purporting also to be executed by his brother, Edgar Oliver.

Starkey, believing that all was right, sold the consols and lodged the relative Power of Attorney with the Bank of England when the transaction was carried through and completed.

Some two years after, when F. W. Oliver had died, it was discovered that the signature of Edgar Oliver to the Power of Attorney was a forgery and that he had known nothing of the transaction. Edgar Oliver accordingly brought an action against the Bank of England for restitution so that his name as the survivor in the joint account might be restored in the bank's register. The bank at once made a claim against Starkey who had presented the forged Power of Attorney to them, and he was made a third party to the litigation.

The case went ultimately to the House of Lords, who found that the transfer of the consols following upon the forged Power of Attorney was invalid, and ordered the Bank of England to place an equivalent amount of consols in the name of Edgar Oliver in the bank's books and to pay to him a sum equal to the dividends which had accrued since the fraudulent transfer was put through.

At the same time the Court ordered Starkey to indemnify the bank by placing at their disposal an equivalent amount of consols and by paying to them the amount of the accrued dividends.

In that case Starkey, who was a mere agent in the matter, was in error in representing that he acted for both the joint stockholders, and he was also in error in presenting a forged Power of Attorney to the Bank of England and inducing them to act thereon as if it were a genuine document. Although he acted quite innocently and in good faith and without any personal interest, he was nevertheless held responsible for the loss arising from the forgery.

From that case you will see that an agent who presents a forged Power of Attorney or transfer to a company for registration will be held personally responsible at the instance of that company for any loss which they may sustain by reason of their acting upon the Power of Attorney or transfer at his request. As you know, banks very frequently present such Powers of Attorney to the Bank of England and transfers of stocks and shares to many companies. Where in cases like that they are acting as agents, they are responsible on the basis of the decision in Starkey's case.

Banks, however, also present for registration Powers of Attorney and transfers of stocks and shares which are drawn in their own favour as transferees, in which case these Powers of Attorney and transfers are presented for registration by the bank themselves as principals and on their own behalf.

In such circumstances the bank are none the less liable to the company for the validity of the Power of Attorney or transfer, and in this connection I would refer you to the case of the *Lord*

Mayor, &c., of Sheffield v. *Barclay & Co. Ltd.* (1905, A.C. 392), which also went to the House of Lords.

In that case certain corporation stock was held jointly by two men called Timbrell and Honnywill. Timbrell, in fraud of Honnywill, forged a transfer of the stock in favour of the bank and borrowed money from them on the security thereof. The bank in good faith sent the transfer to Sheffield Corporation with the usual request to register the stock in name of the bank. The Corporation also in good faith acted upon this request and issued a fresh stock certificate to the bank, who afterwards sold the stock to certain third parties who were then registered as the stockholders.

Subsequently it emerged that Timbrell had forged Honnywill's signature, and Honnywill made a claim against Sheffield Corporation for the amount of his loss. He was successful in this, and the Corporation were compelled to buy in an equivalent amount of the same stock and register it in name of Honnywill and also to pay him the missing dividends with interest thereon.

The Corporation then took the matter up with the bank and sued them, on the ground that they were legally liable to indemnify the Corporation in respect that they had presented to the Corporation a transfer of stock which was not a genuine transfer and upon which the Corporation at their request had acted, thereby involving themselves in loss. The bank were held responsible.

As the general position which emerges on the discovery of a forged transfer having been passed is not too clearly understood, I think I might spend a few minutes in explaining the matter.

A forgery, as you know, is a nullity, and consequently a forged transfer is of no force or effect. If the forgery is discovered while the original transferee is still the holder of the shares, the company may recover the share certificate from him and remove his name from their register. In that case the company's position is an easy one because whatever claim the transferee may have must be made against the person who forged the transfer, or it may be against his agent or representative who delivered it.

The position is a little more complicated, however, where the original transferee has parted with the shares and a second *bona fide* transferee has been registered and a new share certificate issued to him. In this case the company are, in law, barred by their own certificate in name of the second transferee from making any claim upon him. In that case the company cannot get back the identical shares which had been so transferred, nor can they restore the original shareholder's name to the register in respect of those identical shares. It is necessary, accordingly, for the company in such circumstances to deal with the original shareholder in some other way.

As the transfer in question was forged and therefore invalid, the company are responsible to the original shareholder for the amount of the loss which he has sustained through the company passing an invalid transfer of the shares which had belonged to him. His claim may be settled by the company either by payment to him of a sum equal to the market value of the shares plus the accrued dividends, or by purchasing other similar shares and registering them in his name coupled with payment of the amount of the missing dividends.

Naturally, when a company is compelled to

compensate one of their shareholders who has been deprived of his holding through the passing of a forged transfer, the company have a claim for indemnity against the person by whom that forged transfer was presented to them.

That person was either the transferee under the forged transfer or his stockbroker or other agent, and the company's claim for indemnity will be directed against one or other accordingly. The directors of the company are not entitled to ignore this right of indemnity which must, in the interests of their other shareholders, be pressed against the party responsible.

With the view of easing the position of matters and the rights and liabilities of such parties at common law the Forged Transfers Acts of 1891 and 1892 were passed.

These Acts may be adopted by any company, but, when so adopted, do not mean that forged transfers become impossible. What these Acts provide is that any company shall have power to make compensation by a cash payment out of their funds for any loss arising from a transfer of their shares in pursuance of a forged transfer, and power is given by these Acts to the company, if they care, to accumulate a fund to be held in reserve for the purpose of meeting claims in this respect.

The compensation so to be paid by the company is not the compensation falling to be paid by them at common law to the original shareholder who has been deprived of his rights under a forged transfer. That original shareholder has and always had a common law right to demand restitution or compensation for his loss.

The compensation contemplated by the Act is compensation to the party legally liable to the company for presenting the forged transfer for registration—*i.e.*, the original transferee himself or his stockbroker or other agent. In other words, what the Act says in effect is that the directors may compensate the first transferee if the shares are taken back from him, or, if he has sold them, may waive their claim against him without their becoming responsible to the other shareholders for giving up the legal right of indemnity pertaining to the company.

These Acts do not come into operation automatically. They require to be adopted by any company which may wish to take advantage of their provisions, and the extent and effect of such adoption will depend entirely upon the terms of the Minutes which purport to carry such adoption into effect. In this way the immunity which might be derived under these Acts by the original transferee or his broker or other agent may be limited or restricted or may be qualified subject to certain conditions which may, if not carefully expressed, deprive him altogether or in part of that immunity.

As you will realise, all sorts of complications may arise out of a transaction following upon a forged transfer, but the important point for you is that, if you should happen to send in a forged transfer for registration, you may find yourselves deprived of your security when the forgery is discovered. On the other hand, if you should have transferred the shares to a *bona fide* third party whose name cannot be taken off the register, the company will be entitled to be indemnified by you for any loss which they may have suffered— except in so far as the company may have deprived themselves of this right of indemnity against you by virtue of their Minutes adopting the provisions of the Forged Transfers Acts.

You will also keep in view that claims of this description may be made against you after almost any length of time, as prescription will not necessarily begin to run in your favour from the actual date of the forgery.

While on the subject of transfers of stocks and shares I should like to mention one other point which, though not properly coming under the heading of negligence, is nevertheless of importance to you. I refer to the difficulties which may arise when a security is taken by way of a transfer of shares in a private limited company.

As you are no doubt aware, under the Companies Act of 1929 one of the essentials of a company which desires to be regarded as a private one as opposed to a public one is that it places certain restrictions upon the members' right to transfer the shares. Such restrictions may take almost any form, but the most usual is to the effect that any shareholder wishing to sell or transfer his shares must, in the first instance, offer them either to the directors of the company or to the other shareholders at a price to be agreed upon or to be fixed by the company's auditor or by some outside party. In most cases the directors are, in addition, given an unqualified right to veto any transfer presented for registration without assigning any reason therefor.

The position of a shareholder in such a private limited company is therefore very different from that of a shareholder in a public limited company, where there are usually no restrictions on transfer and certainly none in those cases where the shares are dealt in on the Stock Exchange.

The restriction on the transfer of shares in private limited companies will be found in the Articles of Association, and it is therefore necessary before you take a transfer of shares in such a company by way of security to have the Articles carefully examined and see that you conform to the requirements therein laid down. It is also necessary for you to keep in mind that the requirements which you have to meet when taking the transfer are the same requirements which a subsequent purchaser from you will have to meet when he wishes to register a transfer in his favour.

If registration of a transfer in favour of the bank is refused by the company the position may perhaps not be so bad, as the bank will probably refuse to make advances except on condition of the transfer being registered. It is quite possible, however, that the transfer in favour of the bank may be passed by the company, and when an attempt is made by the bank later to realise their security and sell their shares, the transfer by the bank to the purchaser might be refused.

The case of *Stevenson* v. *Wilson and Others* (1907, S.C. 445) is an interesting illustration of what may take place in such circumstances.

In that case Sir D. M. Stevenson had purchased from the trustee on the sequestrated estates of J. & D. T. Colquhoun certain shares in J. M. Smith Ltd. When the transfer was presented to J. M. Smith Ltd. for registration, they refused to pass it. The trustee who had sold the shares, and in whose name they still stood registered, refused to receive from the company the dividends declared subsequent to the date of the transfer and pass them on to the purchaser. The purchaser accordingly raised an action against the trustee as the seller to compel him to do so.

The trustee did not offer to annul the contract and refund the purchase price, and the Court held that if the purchaser was unable to offer a transferee acceptable to the company the trustee was bound to receive from time to time the dividends and bonuses declared on the shares and to account for them to the purchaser. That would not be a very comfortable position for you to find yourselves in either as transferees or transferors, and, consequently, great care should be taken in dealing with shares in private limited companies to make sure that your position will be as safe as possible.

Even where the registration of a transfer of shares in a private limited company is carried through it may be challenged at a later date on the ground that the procedure followed was irregular or not quite in accordance with the requirements of the Articles of Association and that the whole registration is ineffective. Such a challenge may be raised by other shareholders of the company who may have been deprived of their right to receive an increase in their shareholding, or it may be raised by a trustee on the bankrupt estate of the original transferor. A position of this kind was considered in the recent case of *Hunter* v. *Hunter* (1936, A.C. 222), which ultimately went to the House of Lords.

The details of that case are somewhat involved, but briefly what happened was this : A shareholder deposited certain share certificates of a private limited company with a bank along with a Memorandum of Charge in the English form. Later the bank pressed for and obtained a formal transfer of the shares into the names of their nominees.

The bank at the time were warned that the transfer was open to objection as the Articles of the company provided that no member could transfer his shares until he had given notice to the secretary offering to sell the shares at a price to be fixed by the company's auditors and until the secretary had offered them to the other members. In addition, one of the directors of the company had a right of pre-emption.

Notwithstanding all this, the transfer was duly registered by the company and the names of the bank's nominees were placed on the register. Certain actions were later instituted in Court to have, among other things, the original shareholder's name restored to the register in respect of the shares which had been transferred to and were now held by the bank's nominees, on the ground that the transfer and the registration following thereon were made in contravention of the Articles of Association and were consequently void. The Court held that the original shareholder was entitled to have his name restored to the register in respect of these shares. The result was that the bank ultimately found themselves with no security.

In practically every private limited company you will find that the restrictions on the transfer of shares are somewhat one-sided and prevent a shareholder from being able to realise the money which he has invested in the company. Owing to the fact that the shareholder's money is locked up and no dividends are being paid, great hardship is sometimes caused, and the position of a minority shareholder is not a desirable one. In most cases the Articles of Association, as I have mentioned, provide that any shareholder who is desirous of selling his shares must first offer them to the directors or other shareholders, but they rarely provide that the directors or other shareholders shall be bound to buy. That is a serious defect, as usually there is no outside market whatever for such shares.

This hardship has recently been emphasised, and in a number of private limited companies formed lately a special provision has been inserted in the Articles of Association to the effect that the directors or other shareholders to whom any shares for sale may have been offered in terms of the Articles must within a limited time buy them at a price agreed upon or fixed by arbitration, or, if unwilling to do that, then to agree to the company being wound up forthwith. This ensures to every shareholder in such a company the ability, which he would not otherwise have, to convert his holding into cash.

There are other difficulties which may be encountered in connection with shares in a limited company held by a bank either in security or for safe custody to which I should like to refer briefly.

When the shares in question are those of one of the larger public companies it inevitably happens that the bank hold many lots of shares belonging to different customers, and the total of these forms one large holding registered in the company's books in name of the bank's nominees.

It had always been the practice, when shares so held fell to be retransferred or sold, to give back or sell merely the same quantity of shares and not necessarily the identical shares originally transferred to the bank by the particular customer in question.

It would not, in the ordinary course, appear to be any hardship to the customer to get back similar although not the identical shares, and no question with regard to this practice seems to have arisen until 1921 when the point was raised in the case of *Crerar* v. *The Bank of Scotland* (1922, S.C. H.L. 137).

In that case a customer had transferred to the

nominees of the bank a number of shares in J. & P. Coats Ltd. in security of advances, and at the end of the day claimed that on repayment of the loan the bank were bound to account to her for their intromissions with the specific shares which she had lodged with them and that the bank were not entitled to tender to her a corresponding number of shares of the same denomination.

In the course of the action it was found in fact by the First Division on appeal from the Sheriff Court that the bank had credited the customer in their books with a quantity of shares transferred to them by her without making any note or keeping any record of the denoting numbers, and treated them as interchangeable with other shares of the same denomination held by them on account of other customers.

The Court found also that in the transaction in question the bank had acted throughout in accordance with their usual practice, and that this practice was known to and approved of by the firm of stockbrokers whom the customer had usually employed as her agents to carry through the transactions with the bank. Previous dealings with the same customer had been on these lines.

The House of Lords found on these facts that the bank were not bound to account to their customer for their intromissions with the specific shares which she had transferred to them, and accordingly dismissed her appeal, but only because a precedent with that particular customer had been set up.

The general rule of law relating to the pledge of a security, whether over shares or otherwise, is that on repayment of the debt the creditor is bound to hand back to the borrower the identical subject which had been pledged with him in security. On that rule Miss Crerar would have succeeded in her action against the bank had it not been for the fact that on previous occasions she had been satisfied when the bank followed their usual practice and accounted to her for particular quantities of shares which were, however, not the identical shares which she had pledged.

As it was impossible for banks after the decision in that case to rely for their safety on a course of previous dealing with their individual customers, it became necessary for them to make an arrangement whereby the common law rule as to returning the specific security subject would be excluded. The form which this arrangement took is now embodied in the Letter of Pledge which all the banks use. A clause now appears in the usual Letter of Pledge to the effect that the bank are not to be bound to return to the customer the shares bearing the particular identification numbers of the shares originally transferred to them.

That method of contracting out of the usual common law rule is all right in so far as it goes, but I do not think that the banks have carried the matter sufficiently far. This special contract only appears in Letters of Pledge where shares are actually pledged to the bank in security of advances, but the banks hold vast numbers of shares for safe custody and so on which are not lodged with them in security and are consequently not covered by a Letter of Pledge or other special contract. In all these cases banks are subject to the common law rule, and as custodiers are liable to return to the true owners the identical shares which had originally been lodged with them.

In certain cases, of course, banks may be able to answer such a claim for return of the identical shares by founding on a course of previous dealing with the same customer, but that may not always be possible. I would accordingly suggest that the banks should consider getting from each customer who has lodged shares with them not in security of advances a letter or agreement on the same lines as the special contract now contained in the Letter of Pledge.

Various companies, however, have, within recent years, found it convenient to exercise one of the rights conferred upon them by the Companies Act and convert their fully paid shares into stock so that the shareholder, instead of holding, say, 100 shares bearing various identification numbers, now holds £100 of stock which requires no identification number. In the case of these companies it would, of course, be impossible for any customer to say that he had not got back the identical stock which he had pledged or lodged with the bank, but the companies who have so converted their capital do not represent a very great proportion of the total shareholding capital of this country.

Turning now to another aspect of a banker's responsibility—that which is usually classed under the rather contradictory heading of Secrecy and Disclosure. This subject can be divided into separate branches, and I propose to deal with these separately.

To begin with, there is the question of a customer's general right to secrecy about his affairs. It has long been recognised that it is an implied condition of a banker's contract with a customer that, except in special circumstances, the banker shall not disclose his customer's affairs or the details of his account or the transactions in connection therewith. It was obvious that this general rule must have some qualifications, but

266

for a long time there was some doubt as to what these were. The position, however, was much clarified by the decision in the case of *Tournier* v. *National Provincial Bank* (1924, 1 K.B. 461).

The circumstances under which disclosure is justified were there stated to be generally as follows:—

(a) When disclosure is under compulsion by law—for example, where an order is made under the Bankers' Books Evidence Act, 1879.

(b) When there is a duty to the public to disclose—for example, where danger to the State or public duty supersedes the duty of the banker to his customer.

(c) Where the interest of the bank requires disclosure—for example, where a bank is suing a customer or a guarantor for repayment of advances the amount of which requires to be stated in the Summons.

(d) When the disclosure is made by the express or implied consent of the customer—for example, where the customer authorises a reference to his banker.

The duty of secrecy is not confined merely to information derived from the customer or from his account, but includes information of all kinds obtained by the banker in his character as such.

A simple illustration of this is given in one of the text-books. A police officer goes to a banker to make enquiries about a customer. When asked why the information is required, he replies that the customer is being charged with fraud. This information is not derived from the customer or from his account, but nevertheless the banker would not be entitled to make it known to others.

It should be noted that disclosure under compulsion by law does not mean that a banker requires to give information to any Government or departmental official. Such communications are not privileged. The official must proceed under some definite authority—usually an order of the Court.

In this connection and as an illustration I should perhaps explain that a banker is not bound to give information about his customer's affairs to the police or the Procurator-Fiscal on a mere casual enquiry by them. If the police wish evidence from a banker they can obtain authority from the Court to interrogate the banker, and the information must then be given. A banker can, of course, also be cited to appear as a witness in Court and cannot then plead secrecy and refuse to answer questions.

If, therefore, you are asked to disclose facts about your customer or his account you must ask yourselves whether the circumstances are such as to come under any of the four qualifications I have mentioned. Unless it is very clear that they do you will be well advised to disclose nothing.

Another point connected with the subject of Secrecy and Disclosure is the question of giving references. As you know, an enquiry by one banker of another as to the financial position of a customer is a very common occurrence. This, however, is a delicate matter and you should all be very clear as to a banker's position in this respect. Unfortunately the decisions of the Courts are not very consistent on this subject.

To begin with, it must be remembered that a banker, in giving a reference, is in an unfortunate position in respect that he may be liable in two directions—firstly, to his customer, and secondly, to the person to whom the reference is given.

The general rule is that the banker must not be negligent. His answer must be given honestly and according to his actual knowledge and the information in the bank's books. He is under no duty to make further enquiries as to his customer's position.

If the banker, however, discloses facts which as a reasonably careful and prudent man of business he should not have divulged, he may be liable to the customer for any damage he may suffer.

Again, if he should give untrue or misleading information and a person relying on it suffers loss, the banker may be found liable to him.

A banker, therefore, should be careful not to give information which might prejudice his customer and, above all, must on no account give information unless he is certain that it is true.

An interesting Scottish decision on this question was given by the House of Lords in the case of *Robinson* v. *The National Bank of Scotland Ltd.* (1916, S.C. H.L. 154).

The pursuer in this case had become a guarantor for a loan along with two other persons, and in the end had to pay the whole of the debt. He averred that he had been induced to become a guarantor by reason of representations as to the financial position of his co-guarantors contained in a letter written by the agent of the bank to another bank in answer to enquiries as to their credit. He further averred that the representations in that letter were false and fraudulent and concealed material facts which ought to have been disclosed. It was held by the Court that the representations in the letter, although careless, inaccurate, and misleading, were not dishonest, a fact which constituted a sufficient defence where, as here, the relationship of parties imposed no special duty upon the person making the representations to make sure that the information conveyed was strictly accurate.

In the course of his judgment Viscount Haldane remarked, " when a mere enquiry is made by one banker of another who stands in no special relation to him, then, in the absence of special circumstances from which a contract to be careful can be inferred, I think there is no duty excepting the duty of common honesty."

This decision, however, rather conflicts with the opinions in the case of *Banbury* v. *The Bank of Montreal* (1918, A.C. 626), which I shall refer to later, and curiously enough in that case the earlier decision in the case of Robinson was not quoted or referred to.

The position, as I have said, is not too clear, but in my view when one banker makes an enquiry of another as to the financial status of a customer the banker giving the information will not run much risk provided he answers honestly and to the best of his ability in accordance with the facts known to him. He should, however, decline to furnish information which might prejudice his own customer. In such a case it would be the better practice to decline to give any information. It is only as a matter of courtesy and not of legal right that such information is asked or given, except at the request of the customer involved.

There is still another case closely connected with the subject of Secrecy and Disclosure with which I should like to deal. This is the question of a banker's liability to guarantors for statements made to them about a customer's standing.

The contract of guarantee is not one requiring the fullest disclosure of all material facts as is necessary, for instance, in contracts of insurance. Nor is a banker bound to give a guarantor who does not ask for it information as to the customer's financial standing. If, however, the banker is asked for information by the intending guarantor, as may frequently be the case, he must answer honestly and to the best of his ability. In this connection he is entitled to disclose the condition of the customer's account. It has been held that the need for voluntary disclosure is limited to anything which might not naturally be expected to take place between the parties concerned—for example, some very unusual contract between the banker and the customer. On all other matters the guarantor, if he wants information, must ask for it.

These principles are well illustrated in the case of *Royal Bank of Scotland* v. *Greenshields* (1914, S.C. 259). In this case a man Hutchison, whose account was overdrawn to the extent of £300 and who was also indebted to the bank to the amount of £1100 under bills, asked his friend Greenshields, who had no knowledge of the financial position, to guarantee his account to the extent of £300. The latter expressed to the bank agent his willingness to give the guarantee. The agent did not disclose the further debt of £1100 under the bills, and Greenshields, not having asked and believing the overdraft of £300 to be the sole debt, granted a guarantee for the £300.

Later the bank were forced to sue the guarantor, and he defended the action on the ground that he had been persuaded to undertake it under essential error induced by the bank agent's failure to discharge his duty of disclosing his principal's indebtedness under the bills.

The Court held that in the circumstances there was no duty of disclosure and gave judgment in favour of the bank.

The following observations of Lord President Strathclyde are, I think, interesting :—

" Now it is well settled law that the bank agent was entitled to assume that the intending guarantor was fully conversant with the financial position of the customer and was not bound to make any disclosure whatever to the intending guarantor. The only circumstances in which I can conceive that a duty of disclosure would emerge, and a failure of disclosure would be fatal to the bank's case, would be when a customer put a question or made an observation in the presence and hearing of the bank agent, which necessarily and inevitably would lead anyone to the conclusion that the intending guarantor was labouring under a misapprehension with regard to the state of the customer's indebtedness. Nothing short of that, in my opinion, would do."

Another case which I might mention, though not dealing with the subject of Disclosure in the sense I have just been discussing, was that of *Young* v. *The Clydesdale Bank Ltd.* (1889, 27 S.L.R. 135). Here a customer, whose account was overdrawn, induced his brother to sign an unlimited guarantee by representing to him that he was only undertaking a liability of £300-£400.

This misrepresentation was unknown to the bank. The parties met at the bank and the agent produced the guarantee and, without reading or explaining it, got it signed. The guarantor had no knowledge of its contents although full opportunity was given for examining it. The bank later raised an action against the guarantor for £5330, and he in turn brought an action of reduction of the guarantee. It was held, however, that the guarantor must accept the consequences of his negligence in signing the guarantee without knowledge of its contents, and he had to pay. I may add, however, that Lord Shand had something to say as to the bank agent's neglect to read the guarantee to the guarantor before asking him to sign it.

There are several other reported cases on the subject, but I shall not trouble you with them. The principles laid down have been fairly consistent to the effect, as I have said, that in the case of a guarantor the banker does not require to volunteer information as to the position of the principal debtor, but if he is asked questions he must answer honestly and to the best of his ability and correct any obvious misapprehension.

I shall now turn for a moment to the question of a banker's responsibility for advising a customer as to the investment of his money. As you know, a large amount of investment is done by customers on the advice of their bankers, and I would like you to have some idea as to a banker's responsibility in this connection. Unfortunately, however, the law on this subject, like many others, is not as clear as one would like.

Two questions immediately arise. First—Is giving advice on investments an ordinary part of a banker's duty? And Second—When such advice is given by the agent of a branch, has he authority to give such advice and so make the bank liable if anything goes wrong?

The only authority to which I can refer you in answer to these questions is the House of Lords case of *Banbury* v. *Bank of Montreal* (1918, A.C. 626), and the opinions given there, though helpful up to a point, are not very conclusive.

The facts of this case were that a person of the name of Banbury, the plaintiff, went to Canada and stayed in Montreal with the General Manager of the Bank of Montreal—the defendant bank— who gave him a letter of introduction to his branch managers asking them, if he applied for assistance or advice, to place themselves at his disposal. A year later Banbury again visited Canada seeking investments and presented the letter of introduction to one of the bank's branch managers, upon whose verbal advice he invested £25,000 upon a loan

to a company who were customers and also
debtors of the bank. The advice, which was
honestly given, involved verbal representations
as to the credit of the company. The company
having failed to pay the interest or principal,
Banbury brought an action against the bank
claiming damages for negligence and breach of
duty. It was admitted that the branch manager
had no general authority to advise as to investments.

While the actual decision turned largely on an
Act which is not applicable to Scotland and on
special circumstances which were present in this
particular case, the opinions of the judges are
interesting.

Lord Finlay held that " while it is not part of
the ordinary business of a banker to give advice
to customers as to investments generally, it
appears to be clear that there may be occasions
when advice may be given by a banker as such
and in the course of his business." This proposition
was concurred in by Lord Shaw. Lord Parker
remarked that " It would be difficult to establish
that advising on investments was part of the
business of banking." Some of the other judges,
however, differed from this opinion, and it cannot
really be said that the point was settled. I rather
think, however, that if the point came before the
Courts again they would say that owing to the
increasing amount of investments made through
banks the position has altered within recent years
and hold that advice on investments is part of
the ordinary duties of a banker. If I am correct
in this view, then, if advice is given negligently,
liability to the customer may arise.

If, on the other hand, advice as to investments
is considered as outwith the ordinary duties of a

banker, one would think that for a banker to supervise a customer's business would be considered even more so. Yet such a case has been considered by the House of Lords. The case I refer to is that of *Wilson* v. *United Counties Bank Ltd.* (1920, A.C. 102).

The facts were that the General Manager of the bank had agreed on behalf of the bank that the manager of one of the bank's branches would generally supervise the financial side of the business of one Wilson during his absence on military service and take all reasonable steps to maintain his credit and reputation. Wilson ultimately became bankrupt and he and his trustee in bankruptcy sued the bank for negligence in the discharge of their duties and for payment of an amount in the region of £25,000. The plaintiffs were ultimately successful and the bank had to pay.

The supervision of a business is, of course, an unusual duty for a bank, and you will observe that in this particular case a definite agreement was entered into by the General Manager. The question of his authority to do so does not appear to have been considered by the Court.

Presumably if the agent of a branch entered into such arrangement without authority from the bank it would be considered that he had exceeded his implied authority. If so, there would appear to be no liability against the bank in the event of anything going wrong.

As I have said, the situation is not one which you are likely to meet with in practice, but I thought it worth while mentioning it to show the grave responsibility which may be incurred when a banker contracts to perform an unusual duty of this sort.

APPENDIX

Company Mandates by Bank Nominees

APPENDIX.

Not infrequently a bank is asked by a customer to give him a mandate to enable him to attend and vote at a general meeting of a company in which he owns shares, but which stand registered in the company's books in name of the bank's nominees by way of a security for an overdraft or otherwise.

Under normal circumstances such a request is agreed to, as the interests of the bank and the customer are identical, although it may sometimes happen that these interests are in conflict, in which case the bank's wishes must prevail unless they have previously undertaken to act and vote in accordance with their customer's instructions.

The general practice so far has been for the bank to give the necessary mandate to the customer, and, in a case where the bank are holding other shares in the same company for other customers, the mandate is marked as being only in respect of so many shares. This leaves it open for the bank to give similar mandates to their other customers and mark them also, showing the exact number of shares represented in each case.

So far this practice, although probably incorrect, has not given rise to any difficulty, but as the position is somewhat complicated it may not be amiss to consider some of the possible questions which might arise in the case of a company faced with a general meeting called to dispose of business of a controversial nature.

There are three possible positions, viz. :—

1. Under the Companies Act of 1929 in cases where no provision is contained in the company's Articles ; or
2. Under Table A. in cases where it has been adopted as the company's Articles ; or
3. Under the company's Articles in cases where Table A. has not been adopted.

Under the 1929 Act, which applies to all companies now in existence, whether incorporated under the 1862 or 1908 Acts, it is provided that, in the absence of any other arrangement under the company's Articles of Association, each member shall have one vote in respect of each share or each £10 of stock held by him. The Act makes no provision for voting by a show of hands or by proxy, and consequently the only competent method of voting is by a poll, while the common law would enable a member to send a proxy or attorney to the meeting to act for him.

The Act contains no special provision as to the voting rights of members who are registered as joint shareholders. They are all entitled to attend, but they are not entitled to vote separately in respect of their joint holding. Each is interested *pro indiviso* in each of the shares so held and their votes must be expressed as the votes of a single member. Such joint shareholders must, therefore, be unanimous as to how their votes are to be used.

Where a member of the company is another company or corporation, sec. 116 authorises such company or corporation by a resolution of its directors to appoint such person as it thinks fit to act as its representative at any meeting of the

company or at any meeting of any class of members
or of debenture holders.

Sec. 117 (3) provides that at any general meeting
at which an extraordinary resolution or a special
resolution is submitted to be passed, a declaration
of the chairman that the resolution is carried
shall, unless a poll is demanded, be conclusive
evidence of the fact without proof of the number
or proportion of the votes recorded in favour of or
against the resolution.

Sub-sec. (4) of the same section provides that
at any general meeting at which an extraordinary
resolution or a special resolution is submitted to
be passed, a poll shall, in the absence of other
provisions in the Articles, be taken to be effectively
demanded if demanded by three members entitled
to vote at the meeting, or by one member or two
members so entitled if that member holds, or
those two members together hold, not less than
15 per cent of the paid-up share capital of the
company—which in this case includes stock capital.

It will be noticed that this section does not
relate to an ordinary resolution regarding which
the Act makes no provision, so that in that case it
is necessary to have resort to a poll.

In any case, therefore, where the Act alone
is the guide to the procedure, we have the following
position :—

1. One vote for each share or for each £10 of stock.
2. Each individual member, not being a joint holder,
   may attend and vote by any proxy or attorney
   who need not himself be a member.
3. Joint members must act together as one and not
   separately.
4. Each company or corporation member may attend
   and vote by a representative authorised by a
   directors' resolution.
5. A poll on an ordinary resolution is necessary.

6. A poll on an extraordinary or special resolution may be demanded by any three members, or by one member or two members, holding in all not less than 15 per cent of the paid-up capital.

Almost without exception, however, the company's Articles of Association contain some special provisions with regard to these various points, and, as every company frames its Articles in accordance with its own views, it is not possible to say that there is any particular set of rules which could be regarded as applying to all companies. The Articles of Association of the particular company under consideration at the time must, therefore, be given effect.

If Table A. of the 1929 Act has been adopted by the company without modification, we find the following position as regards all classes of resolutions :—

1. On a show of hands every member personally present has one vote. A proxy cannot vote on a show of hands (No. 54).
2. On a poll every member personally present, or represented by proxy, has one vote for each share (Nos. 54 and 58).
3. In joint holdings the senior member alone votes either personally or by proxy for the whole holding (No. 55).
4. A proxy need not himself be a member of the company (No. 59).
5. A poll may be demanded by three members or proxies, or by one or two members or proxies holding not less than 15 per cent of the paid-up capital (No. 50).
6. Each company or corporation member may attend and vote by a representative acting under an instrument under seal or under the hand of an officer duly authorised (No. 59), or by a representative authorised by a directors' resolution (No. 63).

No. 55 of Table A. reads as follows :—

> " In the case of joint holders the vote of the senior
> who tenders a vote whether in person or by proxy
> shall be accepted to the exclusion of the votes of the
> other joint holders, and for this purpose seniority shall
> be determined by the order in which the names stand
> in the register of members."

Assuming that the company under consideration
at the moment has adopted the 1929 Table A.
without modification, the following observations
occur as regards voting in respect of shares
registered in name of a bank's nominees, but
belonging to several customers whose interests
are opposed and who wish their divergent views
supported by the voting power of their respective
shares.

In the case of individual nominees they may
all attend personally, but only one, determined
by seniority as above mentioned, can act and
vote. If the customers are all of one mind as to
what they wish done, such nominee can vote on
a show of hands. If, however, the customers are
not so agreed, he cannot do so, as he has only
one such vote and is not entitled to use it either
one way or the other.

The senior of such individual nominees may
appoint any outside party as proxy for the joint
holding, but such proxy cannot take part in a
show of hands. He may, however, demand or
join in demanding a poll and vote thereat.

As no member or group of joint members can
appoint more than one proxy or representative,
such proxy or representative, or the senior of the
group, if attending personally, requires on a poll
to give effect to the instructions of the various
customers he represents. To do this he may find
it necessary to cast so many votes for the resolution

in question and so many against, and if any of the customers have given no instructions, he will, of course, be careful not to exercise the votes on their shares at all. It is not necessary for any member or proxy to use all his votes or to use them all in one way, but it is incorrect for him to vote only for or against in respect of the difference between the votes of the customers who are for and the votes of the customers who are against the resolution. He should actually cast votes each way in accordance with his instructions, for the reason that, except in the case of an ordinary resolution requiring only a simple majority, the proportion of votes might be seriously affected.

If the shares are registered in name of a nominee company, a proxy may attend and vote on a poll under No. 59, or a representative authorised under a resolution may attend and vote on a show of hands or on a poll under No. 63. Such representative, however, will not vote on a show of hands if there is any conflict of interests as among the customers he represents. On a vote on a poll, such proxy or representative will, of course, vote in such way or refrain from voting as above mentioned, so as to carry out the various customers' wishes.

Where, as under the present practice, several proxies are granted to the various customers interested, the last proxy so granted in point of time is the only valid proxy—the others being automatically superseded thereby, irrespective of the fact that any limitation to a particular number of shares has been marked on the documents. As will be seen above, there can be only one proxy, and any such limitation is thereby rendered invalid.

It will be apparent from the foregoing that the practice hitherto has been incorrect in a bank giving to each customer a proxy marked to take effect only as regards his own shares, as only one proxy can represent the bank or their nominees. On the other hand, if the correct practice is to be followed in every case, it will involve the bank in a considerable amount of time and trouble, and perhaps matters can be allowed to go on as they are unless where controversial business is to be discussed at a company meeting.

The foregoing observations apply, of course, only to a company adopting the 1929 Table A. without modification and where more than one customer is involved. In cases where that Table A. has been adopted in a modified form or excluded altogether, the Articles of Association of the particular company must be read carefully and the provisions therein followed with regard to the various points above mentioned, although they may possibly be more or less on the same lines.

Many companies provide in their Articles that a proxy himself must be a member of the company, and, if such a provision is found in the Articles under consideration, the customer himself cannot act as proxy unless he is qualified as a member by holding another block of shares in his own name.

If the company under consideration was incorporated under the 1862 Act or the 1908 Act, and has adopted Table A., it is not necessarily the 1929 Table A. which applies, but probably the 1862 Table A. or the revised Table A. of 1906 or the 1908 Table A., to which, of course, reference should be made in such a case.

It is a question for consideration whether any warning should be given to a customer who asks for a mandate that it may be of little or no value and may be superseded by another similar mandate granted later to another customer for the same meeting, and that objection may be taken at the meeting to the right of any particular proxy to attend and vote. It might be awkward if the customer on going to the meeting were prevented on technical grounds from acting and had received from the bank no previous warning as to what might happen.

It is also a question for consideration as to whether the Letter of Pledge usually taken by a bank in connection with securities of this class should not be altered to the effect of including express power to the bank to attend, act and vote at any general meeting of any company in any way they may think proper or to refrain from doing so altogether. If, however, such an addition were made, the bank would require to be careful not to act at any meeting at the request of one customer and refuse to act at the request of another.

It is probably desirable that a nominee company should have a standing appointment of representatives in general terms to act at any meeting of any company in which they are or may at any time be interested. In cases where competent under the Articles of Association this, if properly worded, would not affect or be affected by a particular proxy given by a nominee company to a customer, where only one is involved, to attend any specified meeting of a specified company.

It is suggested that each nominee company should appoint representatives to act for them in the districts of other nominee companies in case of need. For example, an Edinburgh nominee company might be interested in some meeting in Glasgow or London and it would be convenient to have a representative on the spot who could attend under the general authority previously given.

GENERAL INDEX.

287

General Index.

General Index

General Index

General Index

SEQUESTRATION—*contd.*
ordinary course of business, 129, 134
payments in cash, 128
security for new advance may be completed within sixty days, 164
security must be ascertained and completed, 165
special ranking for company wages, 122, 150
not applicable to firm or individual, 156
third party pledgor, 160, 180
limitation by, 182
time of commencement in England, 144
title of trustee not completed by Act, and Warrant in respect of—
shares, 166
heritable property, 166
trust deed for creditors, 145
valuation of securities, 157
who may apply for sequestration, 141

SIGNATURE—
abuse of authority to sign, 22
adhibited by other person, 21
death or bankruptcy, effect of, 22, 30
firm, 29
forgery, 18, 252
acquiescence in, 18
joint account, 22
limited company, 32, 78, 240
by director since removed from office, 33
trustees, 25

SPECIAL ACCOUNT—
by guarantor for amount due, 187

SPECIFIC APPROPRIATION—111, 123
affecting security, 117
by creditor—time of, 112
how intimated, 113
not entitled to change after appropriated, 113
current account, 113, 118, 121, 123, 167, 172, 189
limited by agreement, 119

SPECIFIC APPROPRIATION—*contd.*
must be made by debtor at payment, 112
rule in Clayton's case, 113
where change in firm, 116

STAMPING, 74, 161
Bills of Exchange, 73, 75
cheques, 3
deposit receipts, 87
within sixty days of sequestration, 162

SUMMARY DILIGENCE. See Bills of Exchange.

TRANSFER—
of balance to new account, 51, 98, 102, 172, 183, 189, 192
of conditional cheque, 7
title of transferee of conditional cheque, 12
of cheque without indorsement, 12

TRANSFERS—REGISTRATION OF, 252, 255
forged, 254
compensation payable under Statutes, 257
restrictions in private companies, 259, 262

TRUST DEED FOR CREDITORS, 145
completion of title under, 145, 167
consent of guarantor or pledgor, 148
discharge, 146
estate falling under, 145
rights of creditor under, 146

TRUSTEES—
signature, 25
liability for overdraft, 26

VALUATION OF SECURITY. See Sequestration.

VALUE, HOLDER FOR. See Holder for Value.

WAGES—
affidavit and claim, 153
cheques for, 152
preference for, 122, 150

WINDING UP. See Company and Sequestration.

General Index

STATUTES REFERRED TO.

PRINTED BY WILLIAM BLACKWOOD & SONS LTD.